Name: ....

Class: ....

School: ....

Nouns

- Nouns are the names for people, places, and things.

- A **proper noun** is the name of a particular person, place, or thing.

- A **common noun** is any noun that is not a proper noun.

- A **concrete noun** is something you can see, hear, smell, taste, or touch.
- Concrete nouns are a type of common noun.

- An **abstract noun** is a noun (such as an idea, feeling, or event) that cannot be experienced through the five senses.

- Abstract nouns are a type of common noun.
- Other examples include **collective nouns** and **possessive nouns**.

Prepositions

- Prepositions relate one noun or pronoun to another.
- Examples include "to," "from," and "around."

Conjunctions

- A conjunction is used to join parts of a sentence.
- Examples include "and," "but," and "so."

Adjectives

- Adjectives describe a noun or a pronoun.
- Types of adjective include **comparatives** and **superlatives**, and **possessive adjectives**.

Adverbs

- Adverbs describe verbs (*write* **neatly**), other adverbs (**really** *quickly*), and also adjectives (**quite** *pretty*).
- They often tell you how, where, when, how much, or how often something happens.

Verbs

- Verbs tell you what a person or a thing does or is.
- A verb can describe an action, an event, a state, or a change.
- The verb can take place in the past, present, or future.

Past
- Simple Past
- Past Continuous
- Past Perfect

Present

- Simple Present
- Present Continuous
- Present Perfect

Future
- Simple Future
- Future Continuous
- Future Perfect

Pronouns

- Pronouns are the little words used to replace nouns. They can be singular or plural.
- The **personal pronouns** are different for the subject and object of a sentence (see below).
- There are also eight **possessive pronouns**: mine, yours, his, hers, its, ours, yours, theirs.

Singular Pronouns

I (Subject) me (Object)

you (Subject) you (Object)

he (S) / him (O)   she (S) / her (O)   it (S) / it (O)

Plural Pronouns

we (Subject) us (Object)

you (Subject) you (Object)

they (Subject) them (Object)

Aa Bb Cc Dd Ee Ff Gg Hh Ii Jj Kk Ll Mm
Nn Oo Pp Qq Rr Ss Tt Uu Vv Ww Xx Yy Zz

‹uni-› ‹mono-›

unit
unicorn
uniform
monogram
monorail
monotone
unify
unicycle
union
universe
monocle
monologue
monosyllable
universal
monochrome
monolith
unification
monopoly

Put the words in the Spelling List into alphabetical order.

1. _____
2. _____
3. _____
4. _____
5. _____
6. _____
7. _____
8. _____
9. _____
10. _____
11. _____
12. _____
13. _____
14. _____
15. _____
16. _____
17. _____
18. _____

Dictation: ‹uni-› ‹mono-›

1. _____
_____
2. _____
_____
3. _____
_____

"Its" and "it's" are homophones. They are words that sound the same but have different spellings and meanings. Which one should be used to complete each sentence correctly?

The museum is proud of _____ collection of unicycles.

The school has changed _____ uniform from blue to green.

You should go by monorail. _____ the quickest way to the airport.

The union has asked _____ members to go on strike next week.

_____ a gloomy picture because of _____ monochrome design.

"Yes, _____ a huge monolith," the teacher told the class.

This is Dad's handkerchief. _____ got his monogram in the corner.

"_____ a story about a dragon and a unicorn," said the boy.

Parse the sentence and then write it on the wall.

The actor performed the monologue perfectly.

subject	verb	object
	transitive / intransitive	

Work out the answers to the clues and complete the crossword. All of the answers are words in the Spelling List.

1. large muscles, one at the front of each upper arm
2. happening once every two years
3. a two-wheeled vehicle with a saddle and pedals
4. (across) 2 letters making one sound, like ‹ch› and ‹ai›
4. (down) a piece of music for two singers or players
5. the 200th anniversary of an important event
6. to make an exact copy of something
7. a problem forcing you to decide between two things
8. to branch off in different directions
9. special glasses that help you see things far away
10. (across) the number 1,000,000,000
10. (down) a two-sport event (skiing and rifle-shooting)
11. another word for "bicentennial"
12. having two parts or involving two things
13. a fight between two people with pistols or swords
14. two people who sing, play, or perform together
15. able to speak two languages well
16. an early type of aircraft with two pairs of wings

‹bi-› ‹di-› ‹du-›

duo

duet

biceps

biplane

bicycle

duel

dilemma

biathlon

binary

diverge

duplicate

digraph

billion

biennial

binoculars

bicentenary

bilingual

bicentennial

Dictation: ‹bi-› ‹di-› ‹du-›

1. _____
   _____
2. _____
   _____
3. _____
   _____

"To," "two," and "too" are homophones. They are words that sound the same but have different spellings and meanings. Which one should be used to complete each sentence correctly?

Was the pair of binoculars _____ expensive?

A good friend helped me _____ solve my dilemma.

The _____ young singers sang their duet beautifully.

The air museum has jets, helicopters, and some old biplanes, _____.

The _____ roads diverged, with one going _____ the east and the other _____ the west.

A weightlifter has a strong back, sturdy legs, and big biceps, _____.

We bought the twins _____ bicycles for their birthday. Anna's is red and Kay's is green.

The _____ great swordsmen agreed _____ fight a duel.

Parse the sentence and then write it on the wall.

Sam and Seth will be competing in the biathlon.

subject	verb	object
	transitive / intransitive	

‹tri-›

- trio
- triple
- trident
- triplane
- tricycle
- tripod
- trilogy
- triathlon
- triangle
- triplet
- triceps
- tricolor
- triceratops
- triangular
- triplicate
- triennial
- tricorn
- trillion

Write the meaning for each of these spelling words.

trio _____

triplane _____

tricycle _____

trilogy _____

triangle _____

triplet _____

triceps _____

Which of these meanings correctly describes the spelling word?

triple
- A. being three times as large as something
- B. existing as three identical copies
- C. happening every three years

trident
- A. a three-legged stand that supports a camera
- B. a long-handled weapon with three sharp points
- C. a hat with its brim turned up on three sides

triceratops
- A. a three-sport event (running, swimming, cycling)
- B. a type of dinosaur with three horns on its head
- C. a flag divided equally into three different colors

Join the dots to reveal one of the spelling words.

Dictation: ‹tri-›

1. _____
   _____
2. _____
   _____
3. _____
   _____

"Hour," "our," and "are" are homophones. They are words that can sound the same but have different spellings and meanings. Which one should be used to complete each sentence correctly?

I am wearing a tricorn hat in _____ school play.

The lives of three families _____ told in the trilogy.

It took less than an _____ to complete the forms and print them in triplicate.

"_____ acrobats do six triple somersaults in a row," said the ringmaster, proudly.

We _____ taking two cameras, three lenses, and a tripod on _____ next trip.

The trio of musicians will be performing for two _____s.

There _____ three equal sides and three equal angles in an equilateral triangle.

In an _____ we _____ going to see _____ friend in the triathlon.

Parse the sentence and then write it on the wall.

Megan had carefully drawn a triangular pattern.

subject	verb	object
	transitive / intransitive	

9

Definite and Indefinite Articles

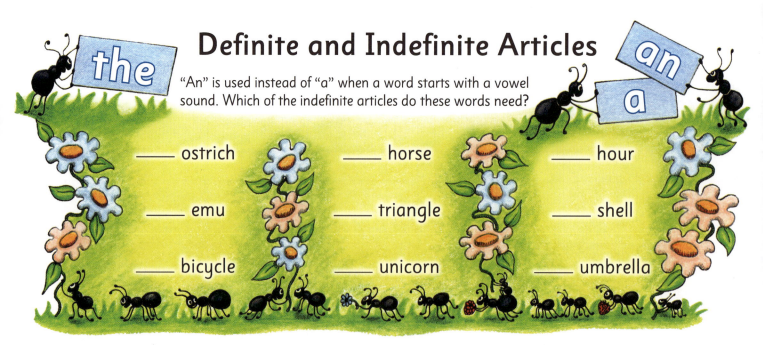

"An" is used instead of "a" when a word starts with a vowel sound. Which of the indefinite articles do these words need?

____ ostrich   ____ horse   ____ hour

____ emu   ____ triangle ____ shell

____ bicycle   ____ unicorn   ____ umbrella

Which article should it be? Write in "a," "an," or "the" to complete each sentence correctly.

I have lost _____ shoe.

It was _____ honest mistake.

_____ triplets are three years old.

Ravi and his friends are in _____ kitchen.

_____ hotel we are staying in is fabulous.

Anna is _____ best swimmer in her class.

They have _____ interesting dilemma.

We are staying in _____ fabulous hotel.

He bought _____ new pair of binoculars.

She really liked _____ kangaroos at the zoo.

Did you walk to school? _____ school is nearby.

_____ funniest clown was riding _____ unicycle.

Action: "The"

Make a capital "T" with your hands, with one hand facing palm down and the other pointing up toward it.

Action: "A," "An"

Hold up your hand, palm facing forward, and point to your thumb.

Definite article   Indefinite articles

Answer these questions, which are all related to the Spelling List.

Prefixes: 4, 5, 6

1. What is a group of four musicians called?
   _____
2. What is a group of five musicians called?
   _____
3. What is a group of six musicians called?
   _____
4. If something is quadrupled, how many times has it been multiplied?
   _____
5. Which five sports are in the Olympic pentathlon?

6. Can you divide the pizza into quarters?

7. How many sides does a hexagon, a quadrilateral, and a pentagon each have? Draw and label them.

8. What is a quadruped? Draw one below.

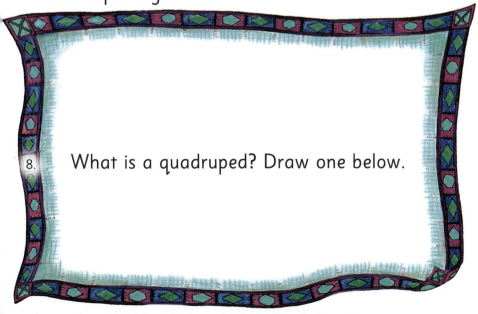

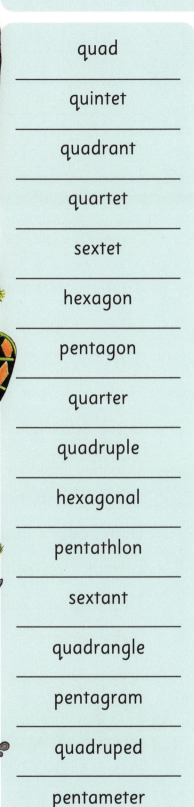

quad
_____
quintet
_____
quadrant
_____
quartet
_____
sextet
_____
hexagon
_____
pentagon
_____
quarter
_____
quadruple
_____
hexagonal
_____
pentathlon
_____
sextant
_____
quadrangle
_____
pentagram
_____
quadruped
_____
pentameter
_____
sextuplet
_____
quadrilateral
_____

Dictation: prefixes

1. _____
   _____
2. _____
   _____
3. _____
   _____

"Your" and "you're" are homophones. They are words that sound the same but have different spellings and meanings. Which one should be used to complete each sentence correctly?

Your / You're playing the violin in the quartet next week.

" Your / You're going to study quadrants this week," my teacher said.

Have you done your / you're homework on hexagons, yet?

Is the book your / you're reading all about quadrupeds?

" Your / You're prices have quadrupled this year!" the angry customer complained.

Didn't your / you're cousin do well in the pentathlon?

Is your / you're room in the building across the quadrangle?

I'll peel and quarter the potatoes while your / you're chopping the carrots.

Parse the sentence and then write it on the wall.

I neatly divided the cheese and tomato pizza into quarters.

subject | verb | object

transitive / intransitive

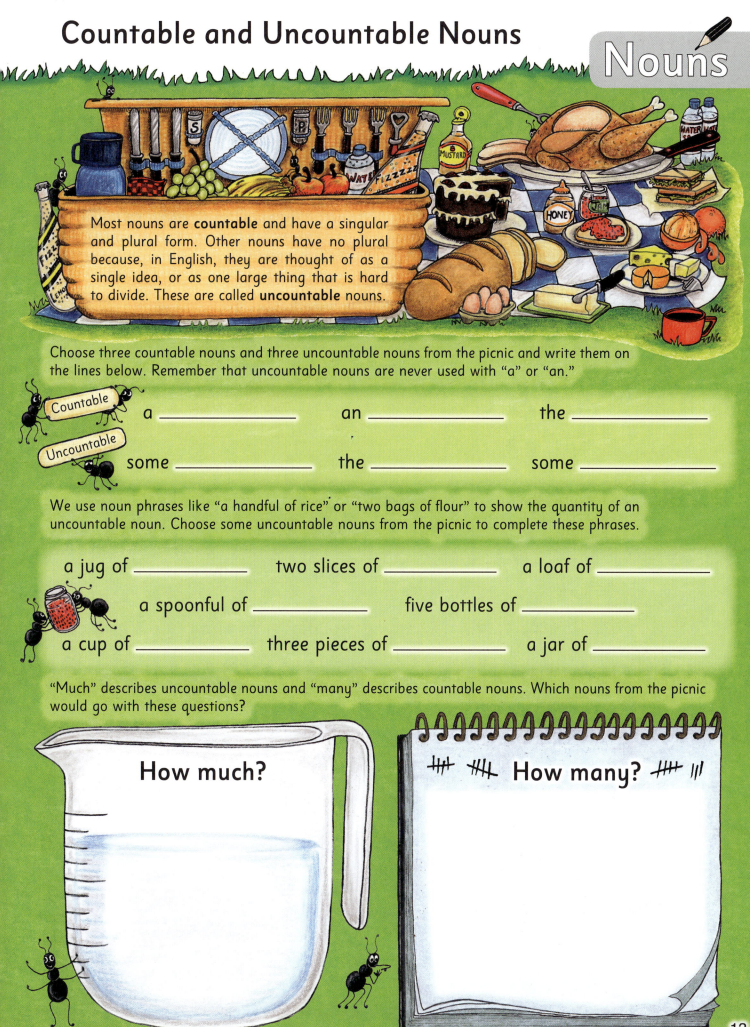

Prefixes: 7, 8, 9

septet
octet
heptagon
octagon
nonagon
octopus
octave
octagonal
September
October
November
heptathlon
septuplet
octuplet
octahedron
septuagenarian
octogenarian
nonagenarian

Answer these questions, which are all related to the Spelling List.

1. What are the prefix(es) for these numbers?

   7 _____   8 _____   9 _____

2. Which three words in the Spelling List are months of the year?
   _____
   _____
   _____

3. How many sports events are in a heptathlon?
   _____

4. Which word describes someone who is:
   70 years old _____
   80 years old _____
   90 years old _____ ?

5. What is a group of seven musicians called?
   _____

6. What is a group of eight musicians called?
   _____

7. How many arms does an octopus have?
   _____

Draw an octopus in the aquarium and then color in the picture.

Dictation: prefixes

1. _____

2. _____

3. _____

"There," "their," and "they're" are homophones. They are words that sound the same but have different spellings and meanings. Which one should be used to complete each sentence correctly?

In music there / their / they're are eight notes in an octave.

The couple have announced there / their / they're engagement. There / Their / They're getting married next September.

I congratulated my sisters on there / their / they're success in the heptathlon.

There / Their / They're are seven brothers in my class at school. There / Their / They're septuplets!

During November there / their / they're will be no concerts in the local park.

Did you know that octopuses have eight arms and three hearts? There / Their / They're really fascinating!

There / Their / They're are several septuagenerians among my grandfather's friends.

There / Their / They're old castle has four octagonal towers.

Parse the sentence and then write it on the wall.

The two small octopuses slept peacefully in their aquarium.

subject	verb	object
	transitive / intransitive	

Grammar Action Sentences

Proper Common
Nouns

Pronouns

Adjectives

Verbs

Past

Present

Future

A / An   The
Articles

Prepositions

Conjunctions

Adverbs

These rows of grammar actions represent five possible sentences. Look at the actions and think of suitable words to make each sentence. Then write your sentences underneath.

_____

_____

_____

_____

_____

Answer these questions, which are all related to the Spelling List.

1. What are the prefixes for these numbers?
   10 _____
   100 _____
   1,000 _____

2. Which word in the Spelling List is a month of the year? _____

3. Which of these sports competitions has the most events: the heptathlon, decathlon, pentathlon, biathlon, or triathlon? _____

4. What do you call an athlete who takes part in a decathlon? _____

5. In Roman times, how many soldiers was a centurion in charge of? _____

6. How is 100% written in words?
   _____

7. Which of these is a decimal number?
   A. ¾   B. 0.75   C. 75%

8. What is a period of ten years called?
   _____

9. What is a period of a thousand years called?
   _____

10. How is one thousand written as a number?
    _____

11. How is one million written as a number?
    _____

12. Are units that measure the loudness of sound called "decagons" or "decibels"? _____

13. Which three words in the Spelling List belong to the same word family as "two"?
    _____

‹dec-› and more

decagon

decade

twice

forty

hundred

December

twelfth

twentieth

percent

centurion

decibel

decimal

percentage

millennium

decathlon

millionaire

billionaire

decathlete

Dictation: ‹dec-› and more

1. _____

2. _____

3. _____

"Where," "wear," and "were" are homophones. They are words that sound the same or similar, but have different spellings and meanings. Which one should be used to complete each sentence correctly?

Where / Wear / Were where / wear / were the hundred gold coins found?

Prices where / wear / were reduced by forty percent in the sale.

The famous actress will never where / wear / were the same dress twice.

My family moved to the country, where / wear / were we lived for over a decade.

Her brother wants to where / wear / were a centurion's costume to the party.

We all tried to guess where / wear / were the millionaire would be staying this summer.

All the decathletes where / wear / were training hard.

You where / wear / were celebrating your granny's birthday on the twelfth of December.

Parse the sentence and then write it on the wall.

May and Daisy are celebrating their twentieth birthday today.

subject	verb	object
	transitive / intransitive	

Direct and Indirect Objects

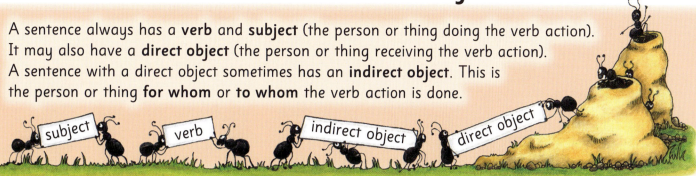

A sentence always has a **verb** and **subject** (the person or thing doing the verb action). It may also have a **direct object** (the person or thing receiving the verb action). A sentence with a direct object sometimes has an **indirect object**. This is the person or thing **for** whom or **to** whom the verb action is done.

In each sentence, underline the verb in red and identify the subject, direct object, and indirect object.

Bill sent his cousin an expensive present.

The little girl sang her granny a song.

Aunt Jill made us some sandwiches.

He gave his mother some flowers.

I wrote my friend a long letter.

Liz threw me the old football.

Dad bought Sam a new uniform.

Miss Beech read her class a story.

We cooked our guests a tasty meal.

Alex and Jo showed Miss Beech their homework.

Rewrite each sentence so that it has an indirect object instead of a prepositional phrase.

They baked a lovely cake for Meg.
_____
_____

Uncle Jim got a new tricycle for his son.
_____
_____

The local farm sells fresh milk and eggs to the villagers.
_____
_____

‹ei› ‹eigh›

- vein
- veil
- rein
- reign
- feint
- weigh
- weight
- beige
- feign
- eighth
- neigh
- unveil
- freight
- inveigle
- deign
- weightlifter
- surveillance
- neighborhood

Put the words in the Spelling List into alphabetical order.

1. _____
2. _____
3. _____
4. _____
5. _____
6. _____
7. _____
8. _____
9. _____
10. _____
11. _____
12. _____
13. _____
14. _____
15. _____
16. _____
17. _____
18. _____

Dictation: ‹ei› ‹eigh›

1. _____
_____
2. _____
_____
3. _____
_____

Write the meanings for these pairs of homophones. Use a dictionary if you need to check.

- rein
- reign

- weigh
- way

- feint
- faint

- vein
- vain

Parse the sentence and then write it on the wall.

The baker has weighed the cake's ingredients precisely.

subject | verb | object

transitive / intransitive

Indirect Objects and Sentence Walls

In each sentence, underline the verb in red. Then identify the subject, direct object, and indirect object. The indirect object is the person or thing **to whom** or **for whom** the verb action is done.

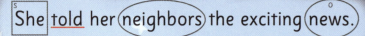She told her neighbors the exciting news.

Bill's father sent him an interesting book.

Dad read the children a bedtime story.

Aunt Jill and Sam threw Liz the rope.

My cousin made me a beautiful dress.

He wrote his girlfriend some poems.

Grandpa bought the baby a toy octopus.

Their grandparents sang the babies a lullaby.

Firmly, the centurion gave the soldiers an order.

The twins immediately took their mother the note.

I patiently knitted Grandma a beige hat and scarf.

Excitedly, Alex and Meg showed Uncle Jim the photos.

Now choose one of the sentences and write it on the sentence wall. Put the indirect object and anything that describes it in the same box, but put the indirect object first and the other words underneath, and join them with a diagonal line.

Add the missing letters – ‹ei› or ‹ie› – to complete the Spelling List words in the handkerchief. Remember, **if the spelling says /ee/, it is ‹i› before ‹e›, except after ‹c›.**

‹ei› & ‹ie› for /ee/

- shriek
- wield
- siege
- yield
- ceiling
- fiendish
- niece
- deceit
- receive
- deceive
- achieve
- conceited
- hygiene
- retrieve
- perceive
- reprieve
- handkerchief
- inconceivable

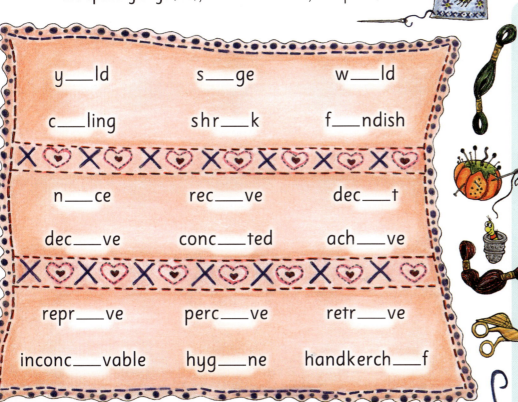

y___ld   s___ge   w___ld
c___ling   shr___k   f___ndish

n___ce   rec___ve   dec___t
dec___ve   conc___ted   ach___ve

repr___ve   perc___ve   retr___ve
inconc___vable   hyg___ne   handkerch___f

‹i› before ‹e›, except after ‹c›, if you want to say /ee/

These words are also missing ‹ei› or ‹ie›. Can you complete them?

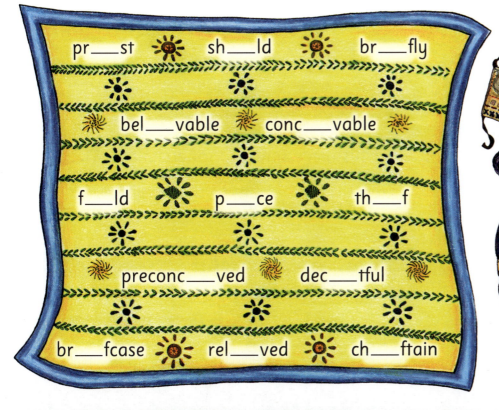

pr___st   sh___ld   br___fly

bel___vable   conc___vable

f___ld   p___ce   th___f

preconc___ved   dec___tful

br___fcase   rel___ved   ch___ftain

Dictation: ‹ei› and ‹ie› for /ee/

1. _____
   _____
2. _____
   _____
3. _____
   _____

When we use numbers to order things, we usually add the suffix ‹-th› (except in "first," "second," and "third"). If the number ends in ‹y›, we replace it with ‹i› and add the suffix ‹-eth›. Write these positional numbers as words.

20 = twenty   twenty + i + eth   20th = twentieth

30th	_____	40th	_____
50th	_____	60th	_____
70th	_____	80th	_____
90th	_____		

When the numbers 21 to 99 are written as compound words, we use a hyphen. Write the numbers below as words.

52	_____	86	_____
35	_____	48	_____

Parse the sentence and then write it on the wall.

Mr. Brown will have bought his niece some handkerchiefs.

subject   verb   object
            transitive / intransitive
                     indirect object

Linking Verbs

Some verbs are "being" words rather than "doing" words. They link the subject to its "complement." This is often a noun or pronoun that **identifies** the subject or an adjective that **describes** it. The most common linking verb is "to be."

In the sentences, underline each form of "to be" in red and identify the subject. Then find the subject complement and underline it in either black (for a noun) or blue (for an adjective). Link each complement back to the subject with an arrow.

They are being very naughty.

The ceiling was incredibly high.

Both actors were rather conceited.

The children had been quite excited.

Those pretty handkerchiefs are a present.

The journey has been long.

You have been really busy.

We will be millionaires.

Our niece is a doctor.

I am a weightlifter.

Other verbs can be linking verbs too. Read the sentences below and decide which linking verb is needed to complete each one. What do these verbs have in common?

The flowers in the garden _____ sweet.

The rabbit's fur _____s soft and silky.

This evening you _____ tired but happy.

Her voice _____s quite young on the phone.

The sandwiches _____ better than they look.

taste smell sound look feel

Parse the sentence and then write it on the wall. Put the subject complement in the same box as the verb, on the same line, and separate them with a diagonal line.

His younger sisters are athletes.

subject	verb	object
	action / linking	

25

‹ei› ‹eigh› ‹eir›

Find the words from the Spelling List. Which one is missing?

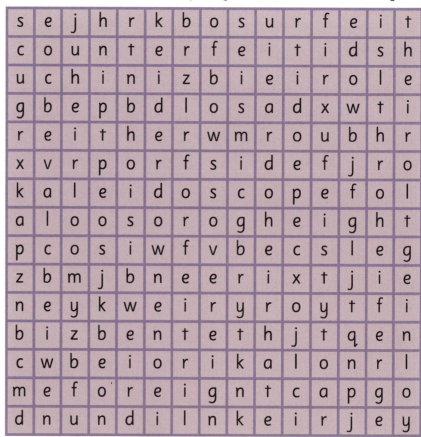

- weir
- their
- heir
- weird
- forfeit
- either
- height
- surfeit
- foreign
- heifer
- feisty
- sovereign
- seismic
- heirloom
- eiderdown
- counterfeit
- kaleidoscope
- Fahrenheit

Which of these spelling words match the description? Use a dictionary to help you, if necessary.

1. **a young cow that has not had a calf**
   A. surfeit
   B. heifer
   C. heirloom

2. **a scale of temperature in which water freezes at 32 degrees**
   A. forfeit
   B. Fahrenheit
   C. counterfeit

3. **a tube with mirrors and bits of colored glass that makes patterns when it is turned**
   A. eiderdown
   B. sovereign
   C. kaleidoscope

Dictation: ‹ei› ‹eigh› ‹eir›

1. _____
   _____
2. _____
   _____
3. _____
   _____

The words below are missing ‹ei›, ‹eigh›, or ‹eir›. Complete each one, decide which sound the missing letters make, and put each word in the correct column.

w____d   h____t   th____   w____   f____sty

s____smic   h____loom   ____derdown   kal____doscope   Fahrenh____t

/air/	/ear/	/ie/

In which of the following words does ‹ei› make an /e/ sound?

beige   either   ceiling   heifer

Parse the sentence and then write it on the wall.

The gold sovereigns were counterfeit.

subject   verb   object
          action / linking

Adverbs

Prepositional Phrases as Adverbs

Sometimes we put prepositional phrases at the beginning of a sentence to make our writing more interesting. Often a comma comes after the phrase, particularly if it is a long one. Identify the prepositional phrases below and then rewrite each sentence so that the phrase goes at the beginning. Remember to add the comma.

I slept peacefully (under the soft, warm eiderdown).
_____
_____

The owl flew off quickly with a short, sharp shriek.
_____
_____

We could see a billion stars in the dark night sky.
_____
_____

The gardens are closed between early December and late March.
_____
_____

The diver spotted a large octopus among the rocks and seaweed.
_____
_____

Prepositional phrases can often be put together to make a longer phrase. Read the ones below, and then think about what might happen next, before completing each sentence.

By the light of the moon, _____

From the top of the mountain, _____

At the bottom of the stairs, _____

During the long hot days of summer, _____

Below the tall trees in the forest, _____

Work out the answers to the clues and complete the crossword. All of the answers are words in the Spelling List.

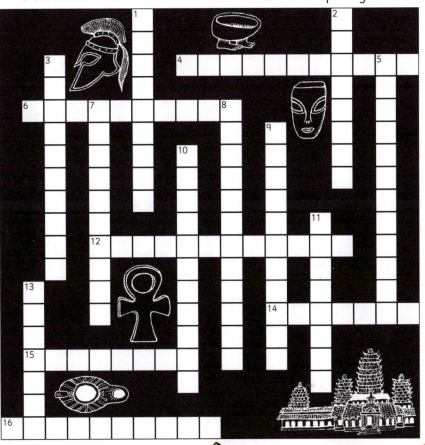

1. a feeling that tells you not to trust someone
2. if you are this, you enjoy being with other people
3. able to do something well or with skill
4. involving several different races of people
5. a feeling of being grateful for something
6. a person's sense of what is right and wrong
7. as much as is needed; enough
8. extremely painful, embarrassing, or boring
9. a person who receives something, for example land or money, from someone who has died
10. not using energy, money, or time in the best way
11. not wanting to be with other people
12. the opposite of Clue 7
13. a group of similar animals or plants
14. very old; existing thousands of years ago
15. the use of force or threats to make someone do something (s)he does not want to do
16. much more than usual; particularly

‹ci› for /sh/

ancient

unsocial

species

sociable

specially

multiracial

efficient

~~sufficient~~

~~suspicion~~

~~conscience~~

~~proficient~~

~~especially~~

appreciation

insufficient

coercion

~~inefficient~~

~~beneficiary~~

~~excruciating~~

Dictation: ‹ci› for /sh/

1. _____
_____
2. _____
_____
3. _____
_____

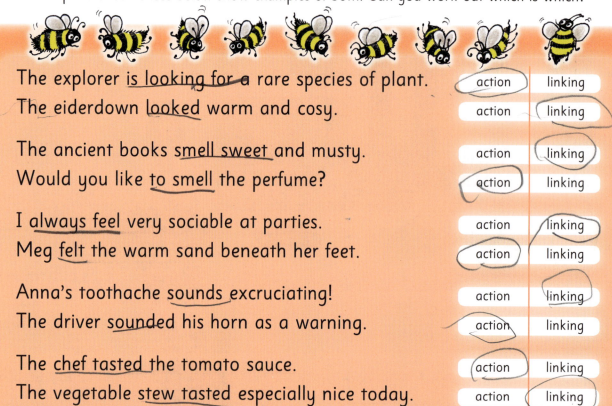

The verbs "taste," "smell," "sound," "look," and "feel" can be linking verbs or action verbs. The pairs of sentences below show examples of both. Can you work out which is which?

The explorer is looking for a rare species of plant.	action	**linking**
The eiderdown looked warm and cosy.	action	**linking**
The ancient books smell sweet and musty.	action	**linking**
Would you like to smell the perfume?	**action**	linking
I always feel very sociable at parties.	action	**linking**
Meg felt the warm sand beneath her feet.	**action**	linking
Anna's toothache sounds excruciating!	action	**linking**
The driver sounded his horn as a warning.	**action**	linking
The chef tasted the tomato sauce.	**action**	linking
The vegetable stew tasted especially nice today.	action	**linking**

Parse the sentence and then write it on the wall.

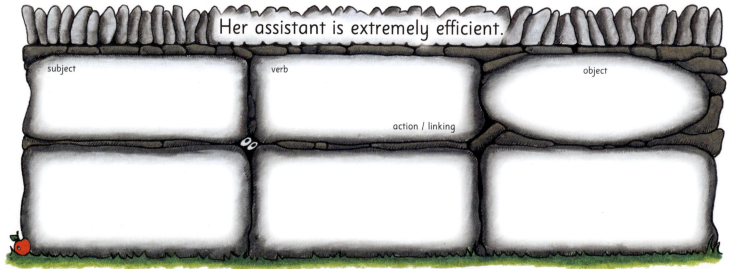

Her assistant is extremely efficient.

subject — verb (action / linking) — object

Prepositional Phrases as Adjectives

Adjectives

Prepositional phrases can act as adjectives as well as adverbs. A prepositional phrase answers the question **Which one?** or **What kind?** when it is acting as an adjective.

Identify the prepositional phrases below. Underline the prepositions in green and put round brackets around each phrase, in blue. Then answer the questions to see how each phrase tells us more about the noun in bold.

The **horses** (in the field) were neighing loudly.
Which horses were neighing loudly? _the ones in the field_

I recently received a **box** (of chocolates.)
What kind of box did I recently receive? _box_

Anna is the **girl** (with the kaleidoscope.)
Which girl is Anna? _____

November is the **month** (after October.)
Which month is November? _____

She gave her niece a **bottle** (of perfume.)
What kind of bottle did she give her niece? _____

The **eiderdown** (on the bed) is a family heirloom.
Which eiderdown is a family heirloom? _____

Think of a prepositional phrase to complete each noun phrase and write it on the line.

the feisty heifer _____
the weird smell _____
the fiendish laughter _____
a pretty handkerchief _____

near the park   inside the box
up the road   under the trees

Think of _four short_ noun phrases and write them on the lines. Then add a prepositional phrase to make each one longer:

_____
_____
_____
_____

31

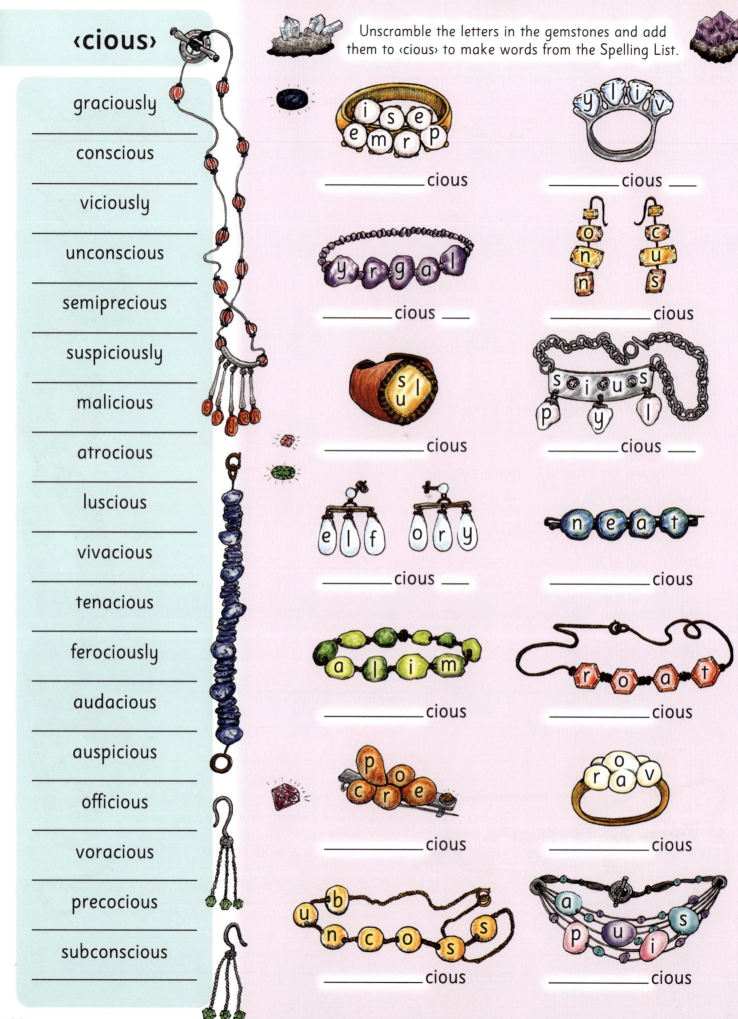

Dictation: ‹cious›

1. _____
2. _____
3. _____

Look this word up in the dictionary. See how many words you can make with its letters.

semiprecious

Parse the sentence and then write it on the wall.

The spiced pumpkin soup tasted delicious.

subject — verb (action / linking) — object

Relative Clauses

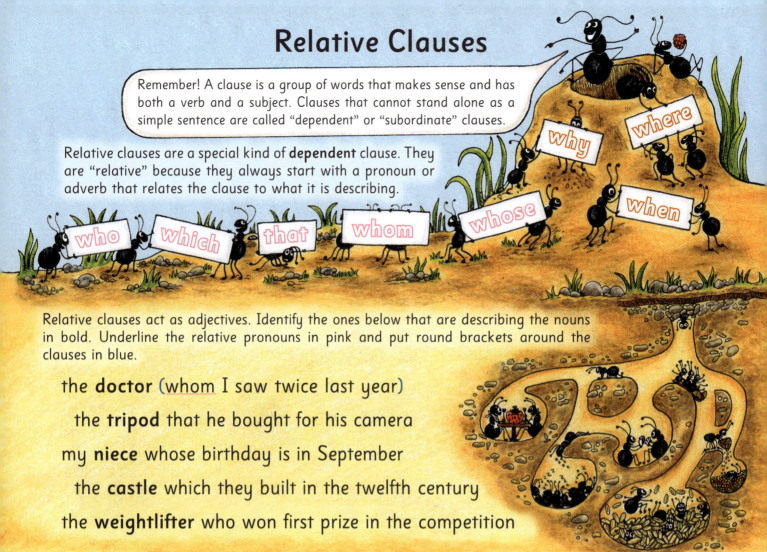

Remember! A clause is a group of words that makes sense and has both a verb and a subject. Clauses that cannot stand alone as a simple sentence are called "dependent" or "subordinate" clauses.

Relative clauses are a special kind of **dependent** clause. They are "relative" because they always start with a pronoun or adverb that relates the clause to what it is describing.

Relative clauses act as adjectives. Identify the ones below that are describing the nouns in bold. Underline the relative pronouns in pink and put round brackets around the clauses in blue.

the **doctor** (whom I saw twice last year)

the **tripod** that he bought for his camera

my **niece** whose birthday is in September

the **castle** which they built in the twelfth century

the **weightlifter** who won first prize in the competition

Some relative clauses start with "where," "when," and "why." These adverbs replace such phrases as "in which," "on which," "at which," and "for which," which are used in more formal language. Rewrite the noun phrases below, replacing the "which" phrase with the correct adverb.

the day **on which** the triplets were born
_____

the ancient city **in which** the treasure was found
_____

the reason **for which** octopuses have eight tentacles
_____

the museum **at which** we saw the foreign coins
_____

the year **in which** she won the heptathlon
_____

the reason **for which** triceratops had three horns
_____

Which of these meanings correctly describes the spelling word?

⟨-eous⟩

1. **bounteous**
   A. an old-fashioned word meaning "very generous"
   B. not relevant to a particular subject
   C. another word for "rude" or "impolite"

2. **spontaneous**
   A. not planned; happening suddenly
   B. happening immediately
   C. happening at exactly the same time

3. **miscellaneous**
   A. helpful or having a good effect
   B. wrong; based on ideas that are not true
   C. including many different and unconnected things

Write six noun phrases using these Spelling List adjectives.

hideous _____

gorgeous _____

piteous _____

outrageous _____

courageous _____

courteous _____

Draw a picture to illustrate one of the noun phrases.

hideous
gorgeous
piteous
gaseous
righteous
outrageous
courageous
courteous
bounteous
erroneous
nauseous
advantageous
extraneous
simultaneous
spontaneous
miscellaneous
instantaneous
discourteous

Dictation: ‹-eous›

1. _____
2. _____
3. _____

Write the adjective and adverb for each of these root words, adding the suffix(es) correctly.

Noun	Adjective ‹-eous›	Adverb ‹-ly›
outrage		
bounty		
court		
error		
pity		
right		
instant		
nausea		
courage		
advantage		

Parse the sentence and then write it on the wall.

The courageous heroes received their medals courteously.

subject | verb | object
action / linking

Relative Clauses in Sentences

There are two main kinds of relative clause. The way a clause is used in a sentence determines which kind it is.

Defining clauses give us important information that helps us identify the particular person or thing that we are talking about.

Without them, the meaning of the sentence would be quite different.

essential information = **defining** clause

If a clause starts with "that" it is always a **defining** clause.

Identify the defining clauses below. Underline the pronouns in pink and put round brackets around each clause in blue. Then answer the questions to see how each clause helps us to identify the noun in bold.

We saw the **woman** (who owns a blue bicycle) in the park.
Which woman did we see in the park? 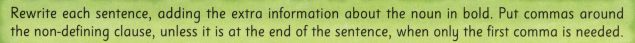 the one who owns a blue bicycle

They have caught the ferocious **lion** which escaped from the zoo.
Which ferocious lion have they caught? _____

They rescued the **man** whose ceiling had collapsed.
Which man did they rescue? _____

The **author** whom you like has written a new trilogy.
Which author has written a new trilogy? _____

The **pie** that my niece is baking smells delicious.
Which pie smells delicious? _____

Non-defining clauses give us some extra information that could just as easily be left out.

We separate them from the rest of the sentence with commas to show that they are not essential.

extra information = **non-defining** clause

Rewrite each sentence, adding the extra information about the noun in bold. Put commas around the non-defining clause, unless it is at the end of the sentence, when only the first comma is needed.

My **dad** especially likes roses.	who loves gardening

_____

I had some semiprecious **stones**.	which my sister gave me

_____

His **friend** is rather unsocial.	whose name is Tom

_____

They would like to visit **Rome**.	where their cousins live

_____

Jenny is coming to stay.	whom they met forty years ago

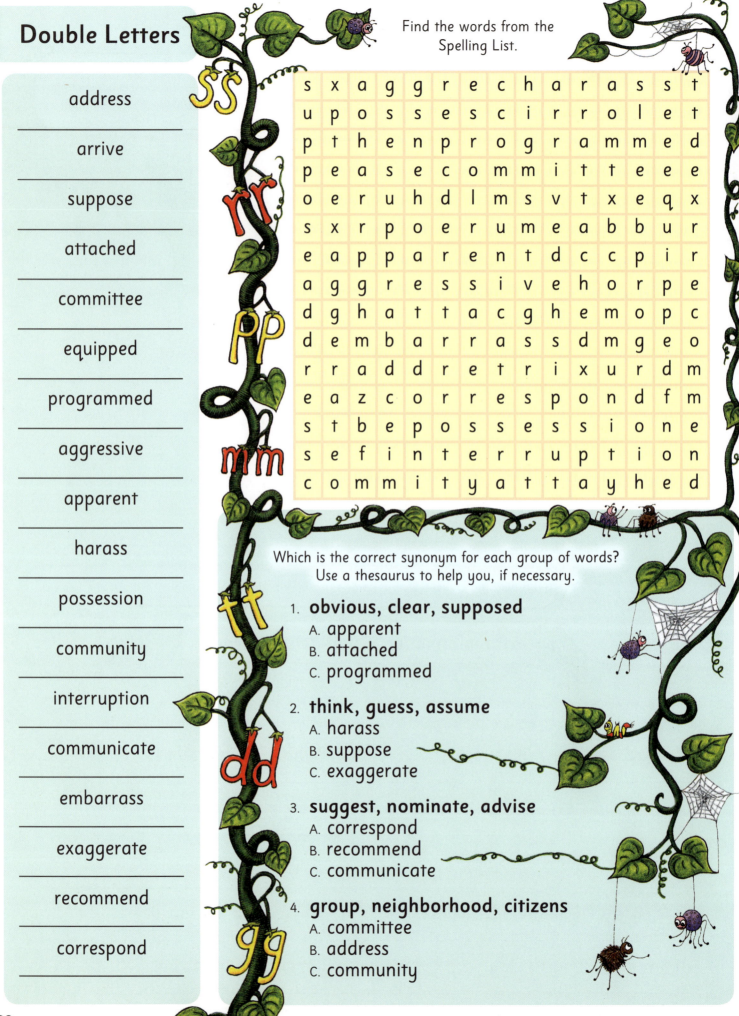

Dictation: double letters

1. _____
   _____
2. _____
   _____
3. _____
   _____

Find the words describing the nouns in bold and put blue brackets around them. To do this, ask the question "Which reason/book/mirror?" etc. Then decide whether they are prepositional phrases or relative clauses. To help you, think about whether they start with a preposition or a relative pronoun (or adverb), and remember that a clause has a verb and subject, but a phrase does not.

the **reason** why we were late	prepositional phrase / relative clause
a **book** about ancient Egypt	prepositional phrase / relative clause
the **mirror** above the fireplace	prepositional phrase / relative clause
the **handkerchief** which I lost today	prepositional phrase / relative clause
a **postcard** from her niece and nephew	prepositional phrase / relative clause
a **suspicion** that something is wrong	prepositional phrase / relative clause
the **storm** in the middle of the night	prepositional phrase / relative clause
the **trio** who sang at the concert	prepositional phrase / relative clause

Parse the sentence and then write it on the wall.

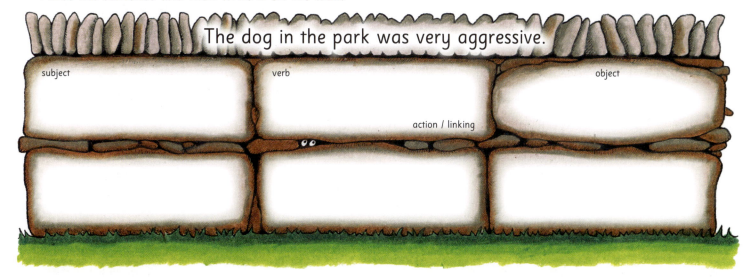

The dog in the park was very aggressive.

subject — verb (action / linking) — object

Conjunctions

Coordinating Conjunctions

Coordinating conjunctions join words, phrases, or clauses of equal importance within a sentence. It is important to use the right one to show the relationship between the joined parts. Match each of the conjunctions below with its correct function.

- adds more
- so
- shows strong contrast
- and
- for
- shows contrast
- shows the consequences
- excludes more
- or
- yet
- nor
- gives an alternative
- but
- explains why

Write in the correct coordinating conjunction to complete each sentence correctly.

Is the patient conscious _____ unconscious?

The tie was hideous _____ my dad never wore it.

His latest book was not well-written, _____ was it especially interesting.

Who is the eldest, your niece _____ your nephew?

I tried two kinds of shampoo _____ I did not like either of them.

For my birthday I got a gorgeous necklace _____ a matching pair of earrings.

They spent many years in jail, _____ their crimes were truly malicious.

The ancient castle is not in France, _____ is it in Spain.

The weather was atrocious, and _____ they insisted on going for a walk.

Those luscious blackberries were sweet _____ very juicy.

It was an outrageous lie and _____ they still believed him.

The money was counterfeit _____ they called the police.

The knight was famous throughout the land, _____ he was courageous in battle.

It seemed like a spontaneous decision, _____ I had thought about it very carefully.

‹cc› for /k/

Write a sentence for each of the first six spelling words.

1. _____

2. _____

3. _____

4. _____

5. _____

6. _____

Draw a picture to illustrate each word.

raccoon

piccolo

broccoli

buccaneer

hiccup

occur

acclaim

account

raccoon

soccer

broccoli

moccasin

occupy

according

accurate

accomplish

piccolo

buccaneer

occasionally

accommodate

accompany

accordion

Dictation: ‹cc› for /k/

1. _____

2. _____

3. _____

Match the independent clauses and join them together with a coordinating conjunction to make a compound sentence.

It was Tom's eighth birthday • • some people believe in them.

The sofa is not especially big • • she was kind and gracious.

Unicorns are mythical animals • • should we wait until October?

Are we going in September • • we bought him a present.

Dad collects foreign stamps • • the children decorated it.

Grandma made a chocolate cake • • he has never been abroad.

The princess was loved by everyone • • is it very comfortable.

Parse the sentence and then write it on the wall.

The raccoons under the house were eating our broccoli.

subject | verb | object
action / linking

Semicolons and Compound Sentences

A semicolon marks the place where we should pause in speaking. Like the colon, it has a longer pause than a comma, but a shorter one than a period. Write a semicolon in each patchwork piece, using a different color each time.

To help our writing flow better, we often join short simple sentences together to make a compound sentence. Usually we use coordinating conjunctions to do this, but when the sentences are closely related we can use a semicolon instead.

Underline each coordinating conjunction in purple, and then rewrite the compound sentences using a semicolon.

She arrived early but her friends were late.
_____

Tom weighed the sugar and Sue beat the eggs.
_____

It was a costume party, so I went as a Roman centurion.
_____

Go equipped with warm clothes, for it will be very cold.
_____

We highly recommended the steak, yet they chose the fish.
_____

Join each pair of simple sentences with a semicolon to make a compound sentence.

I had lost the address. I could not find the house.
_____

The old lady was very poor. She had few possessions.
_____

No one was hurt. The fire had been greatly exaggerated.
_____

Write a compound sentence of your own, using a semicolon.
_____
_____

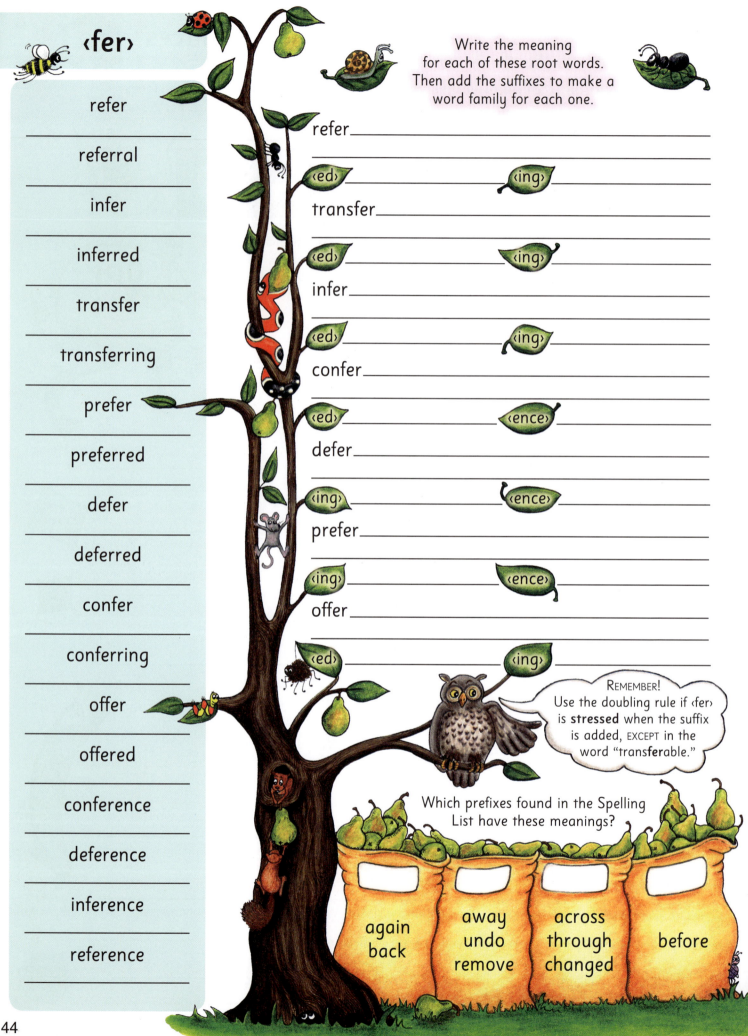

Dictation: ‹fer›

1. _____

2. _____

3. _____

Complete these sentences by making a list. Remember to use a comma to separate each item, except for the last two, which should be separated by a comma followed by "and."

On my walk I saw _____

At the restaurant, the family ordered _____

Sometimes, an item in a list already has a comma, such as "a big, comfy chair" or "a small, low table." When this happens, you can use a semicolon instead of a comma to separate all the items. Look at the lists below and add the semicolons to make them more understandable.

For his birthday, Dad got some socks, gloves, and slippers ◯ a warm, waterproof jacket ◯ and a black, green, and gold mountain bike.

In Sam's lunchbox, there is a cheese, lettuce, and tomato sandwich ◯ some raisins, nuts, and pumpkin seeds ◯ and a red, shiny apple.

The singers in the concert are Marco from Rome, Italy ◯ Kimi from Tokyo, Japan ◯ Nate from Darwin, Australia ◯ and Miriam from Luxor, Egypt.

Parse the sentence and then write it on the wall.

The bank transferred the money to their account.

subject | verb (action / linking) | object

Colons in Sentences

As well as introducing a list of bullet points, colons can also be used in sentences. We use a colon in our writing to introduce things like a **list of examples**, a **single idea**, or an **explanation**. Write colons in the musical notes below, using a different color each time.

Expand these sentences, using a colon to introduce a different list of examples each time.

We need to take the following items on our trip.
_____
_____

They sell many things at the market.
_____
_____

I bought these ingredients for the cake.
_____
_____

Identify which two sentences below are incorrect and rewrite them so that the colon is used properly.

REMEMBER! In a sentence, a colon is only used after an independent clause, and it never separates a verb from either its object or its complement.

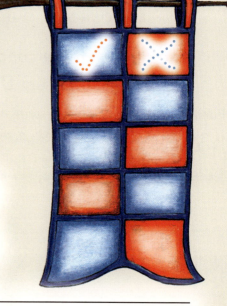

At the zoo I saw: raccoons, beavers, turtles, bears, and many other animals.
   There is an important reason to eat broccoli: it is extremely good for you.
Alex can play several instruments, including: the piccolo, the piano, and the accordion.
   Dad quickly poured me a glass of water: I had started to hiccup and could not stop.
Strange things occurred that night: clocks stopped, the mirror cracked, and the owls shrieked loudly.

_____
_____
_____
_____

Write a sentence for each of these spelling words.

soup _____

fruit _____

movie _____

youth _____

prove _____

suit _____

bruise _____

group _____

shoe _____

juice _____

route _____

canoe _____

Long /oo/

fruit
suit
soup
youth
movie
prove
shoe
route
canoe
group
juice
bruise
wound
recruit
removal
approval
disapprove
improvement

Dictation: long /oo/

1. _____

2. _____

3. _____

Write the name for each fruit and color in the pictures.
Some can be made into fruit juice – which juice do you like best?

Parse the sentence and then write it on the wall.

Robert's little brother showed the nurse his bruised knee.

subject | verb | object
action / linking
indirect object

48

Subordinating Conjunctions

Unlike coordinating conjunctions, which join together clauses of equal importance, a **subordinating conjunction** joins the "main" or "independent" clause in a sentence to a less important "subordinate" or "dependent" one.

A **subordinate clause** starts with a subordinating conjunction and always contains a verb and subject. In each clause below, underline the conjunction in purple and the verb in red, and identify the subject.

because they offered to help
whereas Ben preferred chocolate
while you are painting the ceiling
although she had some interruptions
whether you call it soccer or football

unless you accompany me
until we achieve our goal
when the horses neigh
once we have arrived
if I embarrassed you

Complete these sentences by matching each subordinate clause above to the correct main clause below.

It is the same game _____

I thanked my friends _____

I am really sorry _____

We will not give up _____

His sisters loved ice cream _____

I will be holding the ladder _____

Sam finished her work _____

We can unpack our things _____

Miss Beech says I cannot go _____

The donkeys often bray _____

/ai/ Spellings

Spelling List:
they, prey, break, great, steak, ballet, heyday, fete, buffet, convey, obey, sorbet, sachet, straight, bouquet, gourmet, survey, cabaret

Add the missing letters for /ai/ – ‹ey›, ‹ea›, or ‹et› – to complete these Spelling List words.

ob____   st____k   pr____

buff____   surv____   ball____

gourm____   cabar____

h____day   bouqu____

br____k   th____   gr____t

sach____   conv____   sorb____

Sort the Spelling List words into their spelling groups. This leaves two that have unusual spellings for /ai/. Which words are they?

_____   _____

Dictation: /ai/

1. _____

2. _____

3. _____

Write the meanings for these pairs of homophones. Use a dictionary if you need to check.

- steak
- stake
- great
- grate
- break
- brake
- prey
- pray

Parse the sentence and then write it on the wall.

The great ballet dancer received a huge bouquet of lilies.

subject | verb | object
| | action / linking |

Complex Sentences

 A sentence with an independent clause and a subordinate clause is called a **complex** sentence.

The **main** or "independent" clause has the important information we need to know about something.

The **subordinate** or "dependent" clause provides extra detail, such as telling us more about when, where, or why it happened.

Remember that subordinate clauses always start with a **subordinating conjunction**.

 main clause + subordinate clause = complex sentence

Identify the main clause and subordinate clause in each sentence. Start by identifying the verb and subject in each clause. Then put square brackets around the main clause to show that this part of the sentence is the most important, and underline the conjunction belonging to the subordinate clause in purple.

[Ted drank some fruit juice] after he finished his toast.

I will clean my shoes before I go to school.

Granny hummed a tune as she stirred the soup.

We always eat popcorn whenever we go to the movies.

The route was hard and dangerous wherever they went.

Dad has worn the suit twice since he bought it.

 subordinate clause + comma + main clause = complex sentence

We can change the rhythm of our writing and make it more interesting by putting the subordinate clause at the beginning of the sentence. When we do this, we separate the two clauses with a comma. Rewrite the sentences above in this way.

_____
_____
_____
_____
_____
_____

Work out the answers to the clues and complete the crossword. All of the answers are words in the Spelling List.

"Silent ⟨h⟩" Digraphs

Sikh

ankh

khaki

rhyme

rhythm

Buddhism

rhino

jodhpurs

rhubarb

rhombus

rhapsody

sheikh

dhoti

sadhu

gymkhana

rhinoceros

rheumatism

rhythmically

1. an ancient Egyptian symbol, meaning "life"
2. music and dance can be performed in this way
3. a religion, originally from east and central Asia
4. a strong pattern of sounds or movements that is repeated regularly
5. a day of horse racing and jumping competitions
6. a member of a religious group, founded in India
7. a disease that makes your joints stiff and painful
8. an Arab prince, ruler, or chief
9. a traditional Indian garment, worn by men
10. a shape like a square but with sloping sides
11. a Hindu holy man who lives a very simple life
12. a light shade of yellow-brown or green-brown
13. another word for a short poem or verse
14. special trousers sometimes worn when riding horses
15. a piece of classical music expressing great emotion
16. thick red plant stems that can be cooked and eaten
17. a shorter way of saying Clue 18
18. a very big animal with one or two horns on its nose

Dictation: silent ‹h›

1. _____

2. _____

3. _____

Can you think of any words that rhyme with the ones below? Write an example for each one.

sheikh	suit	prey	arrive
acclaim	confer	canoe	rhyme
preferred	address	straight	buccaneer

Now try writing a short poem using some of these rhyming words.

Parse the sentence and then write it on the wall.

Dad has bought the khaki shorts with the big pockets.

subject | verb | object

action / linking

Simple, Compound, and Complex Sentences

A **simple** sentence (or "independent clause") has a verb and a subject. It expresses a complete thought.
A **compound** sentence has two independent clauses, joined by a coordinating conjunction or a semicolon.
A **complex** sentence has a main (or "independent") clause, plus a subordinate (or "dependent") clause that starts with a subordinating conjunction or with a relative pronoun or adverb.

Are these sentences simple, compound, or complex? Underline any conjunctions in purple, and put square brackets around the independent clauses. Then circle the answer you think is correct.

REMEMBER! If there is only an independent clause, circle "simple."

If there are two clauses joined by one of the FANBOYS conjunctions (for, and, nor, but, or, yet, so), circle "compound."

If there are two clauses and the one starting with the conjunction can be moved to the beginning of the sentence, circle "complex."

You are wrong and I can prove it.	simple · compound · complex
It was a cold day so Grandma made some soup.	simple · compound · complex
The children paddled their canoes down the river.	simple · compound · complex
They took umbrellas because it was raining.	simple · compound · complex
I am really tired now but I had a great time.	simple · compound · complex
The dog obeyed whenever Jack said, "Sit."	simple · compound · complex
Uncle Jim loves steak with mashed potatoes.	simple · compound · complex
Joe likes ice cream, yet he has never tried sorbet.	simple · compound · complex
Do you want fruit or would you prefer chocolate?	simple · compound · complex
Sally bruised her knee when she fell off her bike.	simple · compound · complex
The new gourmet restaurant is very expensive.	simple · compound · complex
Both the twins are doing ballet this year.	simple · compound · complex
I went straight home before it got dark.	simple · compound · complex
You will be in trouble if you break anything.	simple · compound · complex
We gave Sue a bouquet of flowers for her birthday.	simple · compound · complex

/t/ Spellings

- debt
- doubt
- paste
- baste
- thyme
- Thailand
- yacht
- subtle
- rosette
- palette
- definite
- favorite
- suite
- baguette
- statuette
- brunette
- silhouette
- redoubtable

Write the meaning for each of these spelling words.

debt _____

doubt _____

paste _____

thyme _____

Thailand _____

palette _____

brunette _____

silhouette _____

Draw a picture to illustrate each word.

yacht

rosette

baguette

statuette

Dictation: /t/

1. _____

2. _____

3. _____

Think of a main clause to go with each subordinate clause to make a complex sentence. Write the sentence down and remember to add a comma after the subordinate clause if it goes at the beginning. What does the subordinate clause tell us about the main clause?

after our trip to Thailand   explains | contrasts | makes conditional | says when
_____
_____

although I had some doubts   explains | contrasts | makes conditional | says when
_____
_____

unless you pay your debts   explains | contrasts | makes conditional | says when
_____
_____

because the yacht was very fast   explains | contrasts | makes conditional | says when
_____
_____

Parse the sentence and then write it on the wall.

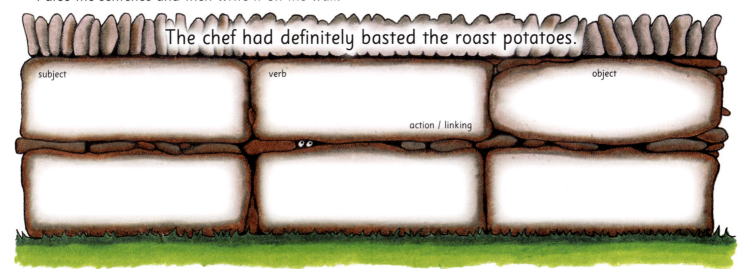

The chef had definitely basted the roast potatoes.

subject | verb | object
action / linking

Adverbs

Adverbials

An **adverbial** is any word, phrase, or clause that acts as an adverb in a sentence. The most common adverbials are adverbs, noun phrases, prepositional phrases, and subordinate clauses. They tell us more about, for example, **where**, **when**, **how,** or **why** the verb is happening.

Identify the adverbial in each sentence and put orange brackets around it. Then decide what the adverbial is telling us about the verb.

I drank some water (because I had the hiccups).	How? • Where? • When? • (Why?)
Tom carefully drew a square and a rhombus.	How? • Where? • When? • Why?
They had rhubarb and custard on Tuesday.	How? • Where? • When? • Why?
The hungry wolf hunted its prey in silence.	How? • Where? • When? • Why?
Grandpa wears a suit wherever he goes.	How? • Where? • When? • Why?
There will be a gymkhana next month.	How? • Where? • When? • Why?
Grandma has rheumatism in her hands.	How? • Where? • When? • Why?
The zoo received a white rhino last year.	How? • Where? • When? • Why?
Anna wore her khaki shorts at the beach.	How? • Where? • When? • Why?
I got some new moccasins for my birthday.	How? • Where? • When? • Why?
The little brown crickets chirped rhythmically.	How? • Where? • When? • Why?
We loved nursery rhymes when we were young.	How? • Where? • When? • Why?

An adverbial that begins a sentence is called a **fronted adverbial**. We usually use a comma to separate a fronted adverbial from the rest of the sentence. Choose six of the sentences above and rewrite them so the adverbial is at the beginning, followed by a comma.

_____

_____

_____

_____

_____

Write a sentence for each of these spelling words.

/m/ Spellings

numb _____

hymn _____

welcome _____

column _____

solemn _____

condemn _____

gruesome _____

handsome _____

honeycomb _____

numb
bomb
come
some
hymn
autumn
welcome
column
dumb
solemn
condemn
gruesome
income
outcome
handsome
thumbnail
tombstone
honeycomb

Can you find the compound words in the Spelling List? Write three of them in the birds below.

Dictation: /m/

1. _____

2. _____

3. _____

Think of an antonym and a synonym for each word.

REMEMBER! **Antonyms** are words that have the opposite meaning...

antonym

...and **synonyms** are words which have the same, or a similar, meaning.

synonym

	antonym	synonym
gruesome		
doubt		
great		
welcome		
come		
accurate		
solemn		
handsome		

Parse the sentence and then write it on the wall.

The committee gave the musicians a courteous welcome.

subject | verb | object
 | action / linking |
 | | indirect object

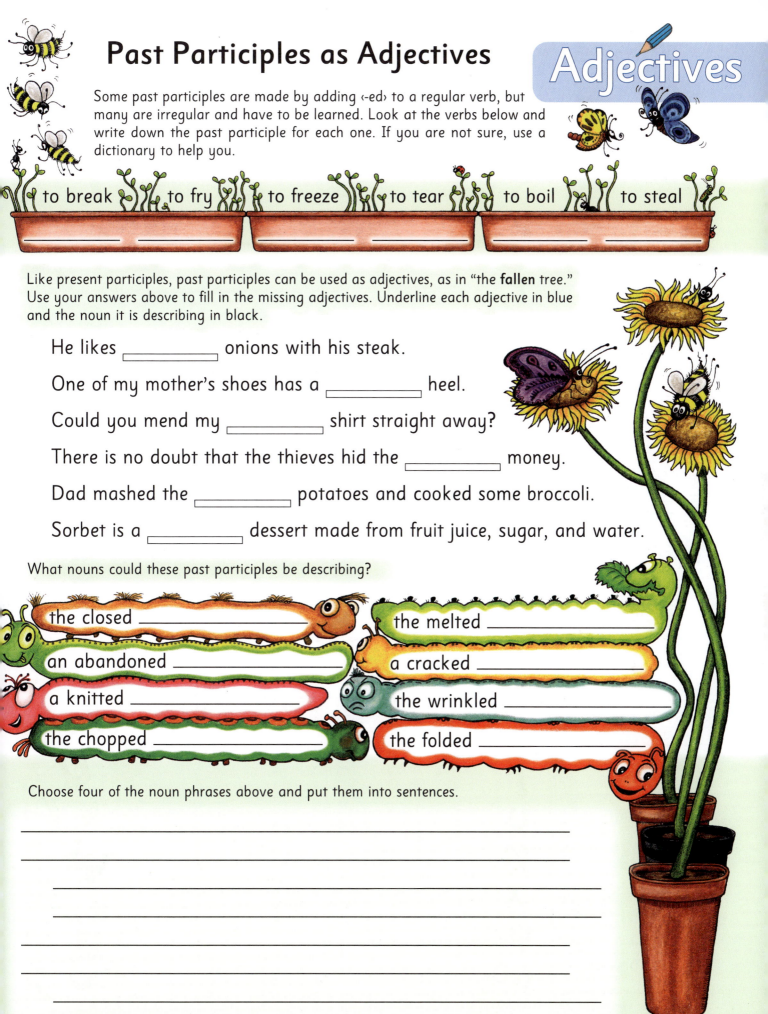

"Silent ‹p›" Digraphs

psalm
psyche
pseudo
tempt
prompt
attempt
receipt
pneumonia
pneumatic
psychiatry
psychology
pterodactyl
psychiatrist
pseudonym
ptarmigan
psoriasis
psi
psychological

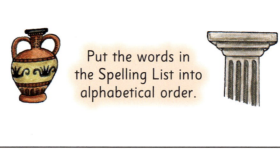

Put the words in the Spelling List into alphabetical order.

1. _____
2. _____
3. _____
4. _____
5. _____
6. _____
7. _____
8. _____
9. _____
10. _____
11. _____
12. _____
13. _____
14. _____
15. _____
16. _____
17. _____
18. _____

Dictation: silent ‹p›

1. _____
2. _____
3. _____

Check what this word means and see how many other words you can make with its letters.

p s y c h o l o g i c a l

Parse the sentence and then write it on the wall.

The psoriasis on the patient's arm looked rather sore.

subject | verb | object
| | action / linking |

The Active and Passive Voice

When the subject of a sentence is doing the verb action, we are writing in the **active** voice.

subject **doing** verb action (+ object) = **active** voice
subject **receiving** verb action (+ "by" + agent) = **passive** voice

When we do not know who is doing the verb action, or we think that the object is more important, we can rewrite the sentence in the **passive** voice.

We do this by turning the object into the subject and by using the verb "to be" with the past participle.

Decide which of the sentences in each pair is written in the active voice and which is written in the passive. Start by identifying the verb and subject. Then think about whether the subject is doing the verb action or receiving it.

The yacht was sailed by the crew. — active • passive
The crew sailed the yacht. — active • passive

Bees store honey in a honeycomb. — active • passive
Honey is stored in a honeycomb. — active • passive

We welcomed our guests to the party. — active • passive
Our guests were welcomed to the party. — active • passive

Some seeds will be planted by the gardener. — active • passive
The gardener will plant some seeds. — active • passive

Are these sentences active or passive? Identify the verb and subject in each one and circle the answer you think is correct.

A hymn was sung by the choir. — active • passive
Sam bruised his knee in the park. — active • passive
Rhinos come from Africa and Asia. — active • passive
The chicken was basted by the cook. — active • passive
The autumn leaves fell to the ground. — active • passive
A rosette was awarded to the winner. — active • passive
The toothpaste is kept in the bathroom. — active • passive
Lucy went to the gymkhana last Saturday. — active • passive
The baguettes are made early in the morning. — active • passive
Granny gave Anna some jodhpurs for her birthday. — active • passive

Find the words from the Spelling List.

‹ui› and ‹u› for /i/

- build
- built
- busy
- busily
- biscuit
- rebuilt
- lettuce
- minute
- builder
- building
- cuisine
- business
- built-in
- circuit
- busybody
- businesslike
- outbuilding
- bodybuilder

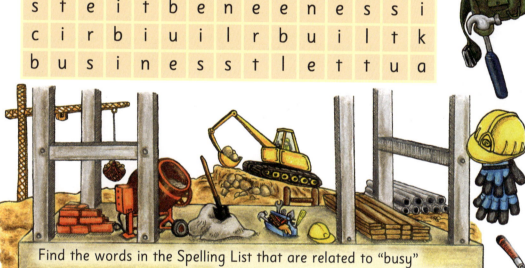

Find the words in the Spelling List that are related to "busy" and write them in the word family tree.

busy

Dictation: ⟨ui⟩ and ⟨u⟩ for /i/

1. _____

2. _____

3. _____

Write the comparative and superlative for each adjective below, starting with "busy."

Adjective	Comparative	Superlative
busy		
straight		
subtle		
numb		
great		
feisty		
weird		
prompt		
handsome		

Parse the sentence and then write it on the wall.

The ancient buildings were built in the twelfth century.

subject — verb (active / passive) — object

The Passive Voice

REMEMBER! When we write in the passive voice, the "receiver" of the verb action becomes the **subject** and the "doer" of the verb (if it is known) becomes the **agent**.

In each sentence, underline the verb in red and draw boxes around the subject and agent, putting either a small ‹s› (for "subject") or a small ‹a› (for "agent") in the corner. Then rewrite the sentences in the active voice, turning the agent back into the subject.

An old [palette]⟨s⟩ was used by the [painter]⟨a⟩.
The painter used an old palette.

The bride's bouquet was made by my cousin.
_____

The bronze statuette was bought by her friend.
_____

The handsome brown horse was sold by the farmer.
_____

The ancient Greek temple was supported by many columns.
_____

The sentences below are written first in the active voice and then in the passive. Choose the correct form of "to be" each time to complete the passive sentence.

We **are painting** the ceiling.
The ceiling am being / are being / **is being** painted by us.

Grandpa **visits** us twice a week.
We am / **are** / is visited by Grandpa twice a week.

A loud noise **interrupted** the conference.
The conference **was** / were interrupted by a loud noise.

A grizzly bear **has wounded** two ramblers.
Two ramblers **have been** / has been wounded by a grizzly bear.

The chocolate chip cookies **were tempting** me.
I **was being** / were being tempted by the chocolate chip cookies.

‹gh› ‹gue›

dinghy

rogue

plague

vague

league

ghastly

meringue

intrigue

tongue

fatigue

spaghetti

ghostwriter

colleague

dialogue

prologue

epilogue

harangue

ghoulishly

Unscramble the letters in the meringues to make the first twelve words from the Spelling List.

Dictation: ‹gh› ‹gue›

1. _____
   _____
2. _____
   _____
3. _____
   _____

Which sentence in each pair is written in the active voice and which is written in the passive? Start by identifying the verb and subject. Then think about whether the subject is doing the verb action or receiving it.

The brick wall has been completed by the busy builders.	active	passive
The busy builders have completed the brick wall.	active	passive
A pterodactyl fossil was discovered by the local farmer.	active	passive
The local farmer discovered a pterodactyl fossil.	active	passive
Arthur grows the best rhubarb in the village.	active	passive
The best rhubarb in the village is grown by Arthur.	active	passive
The handsome stranger intrigued my friends.	active	passive
My friends were intrigued by the handsome stranger.	active	passive
The dialogue for the play is being learned by the actors.	active	passive
The actors are learning the dialogue for the play.	active	passive
Granny will make a delicious lemon meringue pie.	active	passive
A delicious lemon meringue pie will be made by Granny.	active	passive

Parse the sentence and then write it on the wall.

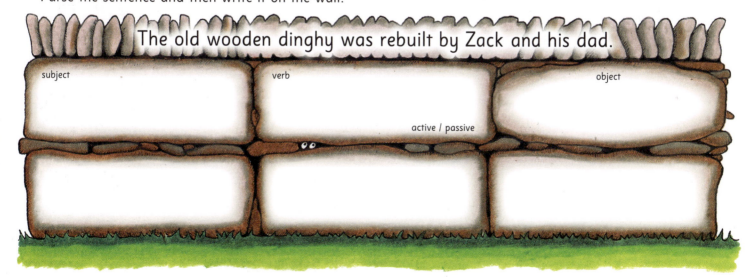

The old wooden dinghy was rebuilt by Zack and his dad.

subject   verb   object

active / passive

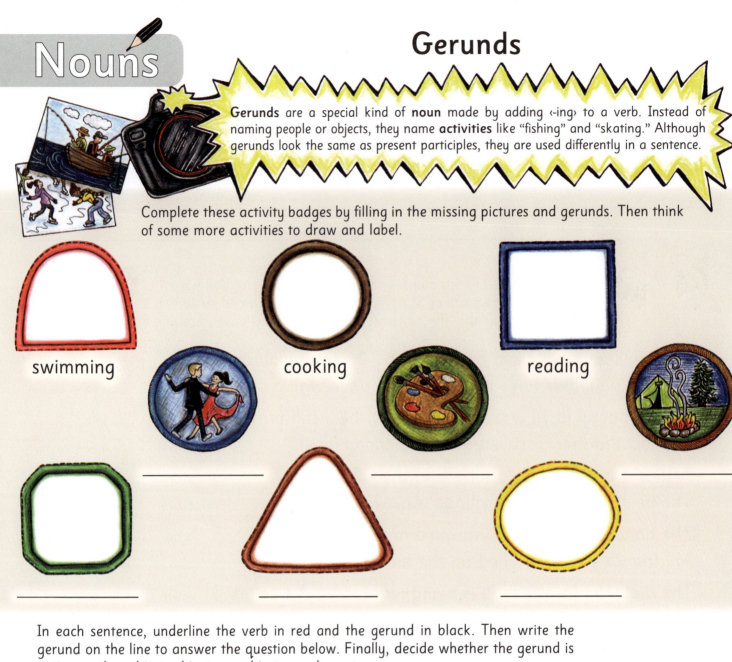

Work out the answers to the clues and complete the crossword.
All of the answers are words in the Spelling List.

‹gu›

guide

guard

guess

guest

guilt

guitar

language

penguin

iguana

anguish

extinguish

distinguished

guarantee

lifeguard

disguise

beguile

guardian

guillotine

1. (across) to try to answer a question when you are not sure you will be right
1. (down) a strong feeling of shame and regret
2. the use of words to communicate
3. to promise something will be done or will happen
4. a person you have invited to stay at your home
5. a musical instrument, usually with six strings
6. extreme pain or suffering of the body or mind
7. admired, respected, and successful
8. this person's job is to help swimmers in danger
9. to hide your identity by changing your appearance
10. to stop a fire burning or a light shining
11. a large tropical American lizard
12. someone who guards or protects something
13. to charm people, often in order to trick them
14. to watch a prisoner to stop them escaping
15. this person's job is to show a place to visitors
16. a large black and white sea bird that cannot fly
17. a machine used in the past to cut people's heads off

Dictation: ‹gu›

1. _____

2. _____

3. _____

The present participle is used with the auxiliary verb "to be" in the continuous tenses. A gerund is a special type of noun that names an activity. Add ‹-ing› to the verbs below, using the spelling rules, and fill in the gaps. Underline the present participles in red and the gerunds in black.

verb + ing = present participle or gerund

verb	present participle	gerund
write	I am _____ a long letter.	The students' _____ is neat.
play	Will you be _____ the guitar?	Little kittens enjoy _____.
swim	The penguins were _____.	_____ is a popular sport.
cook	Dad is _____ spaghetti.	Jane's _____ smells great.
garden	I was _____ this morning.	Jim does a lot of _____.
cycle	They were _____ very fast.	Fred is really good at _____.
shop	We were _____ for new shoes.	They will do the _____.
study	We are _____ French today.	Have you done any _____?

Parse the sentence and then write it on the wall.

Ben quickly extinguished the flames from the fire.

subject | verb | object

active / passive

 # Idioms

Idioms are common expressions that add variety and interest to our language. Every idiom has a special meaning that needs to be learned. Look at each one below and draw a picture of what the words actually say. Then write the real meaning of the idiom next to it.

at the drop of a hat

to bark up the wrong tree

under the weather

to hold your tongue

once in a blue moon

to let the cat out of the bag

73

‹ough›

- cough
- dough
- bough
- rough
- tough
- bought
- though
- through
- enough
- drought
- although
- doughnut
- sought
- thorough
- throughout
- overwrought
- breakthrough
- afterthought

One of the trickiest spellings in English is ‹ough›, because it can say a number of different sounds. Match the Spelling List words to the sounds below.

/uff/
/ou/
/o/
/oa/
/off/
/oo/

Which sound does ‹ough› make in the "tricky" pasts below, and how would you write them in the present tense? If you're not sure, look them up in a dictionary; then write the answers in the wheelbarrow.

ough

bought
brought
fought
sought
thought

Dictation: ‹ough›

1. _____

2. _____

3. _____

Write the meanings for these pairs of homophones. Use a dictionary if you need to check.

- doe
- dough
- plain
- plane
- guessed
- guest
- bow
- bough

Parse the sentence and then write it on the wall.

The thoughtless man coughed loudly throughout the play.

subject | verb | object

active / passive

Verbs

"To Do"

	Past	Present	Future
Simple Tense	I did	I do / It does	I shall do
Continuous Tense	I was doing	I am doing	I shall be doing
Perfect Tense	I had done	I have done	I shall have done

Find the different forms of "to do" in the sentences and underline them in red. Then identify the tense for each one.

You <u>will be doing</u> your homework tonight.

They had done the crossword together.

I did the dishes every night last week.

Anna is doing gymnastics this year.

Jonathon has done nothing all day.

She will have done a very good job.

They will do the shopping tomorrow.

We were doing the laundry this morning.

Dad never does the cooking on Saturdays.

Is it **do**, **does**, or **did**? Write in the correct word to complete each sentence.

The children _____ lots of work yesterday.

We _____ some exercise in the park last week.

The fallen tree _____ a lot of damage last night.

Tom always _____ his teeth before he goes to bed.

Nowadays, Grandma _____ the gardening less often.

I _____ my hair every morning before I leave the house.

Can you think of other verbs or phrases that could be used instead of "to do" in these sentences?

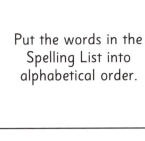 

Put the words in the Spelling List into alphabetical order.

Schwa ‹ure›

picture
nature
injure
lecture
texture
pasture
sculpture
creature
stature
torture
rupture
cultured
manufacture
adventurer
procedure
treasurer
acupuncture
disfigurement

1. _____
2. _____
3. _____
4. _____
5. _____
6. _____
7. _____
8. _____
9. _____
10. _____
11. _____
12. _____
13. _____
14. _____
15. _____
16. _____
17. _____
18. _____

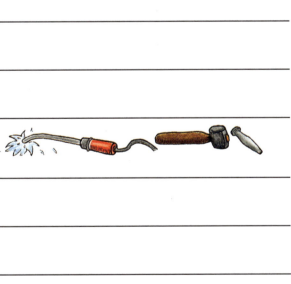

77

Dictation: schwa ‹ure›

1. _____
_____
2. _____
_____
3. _____
_____

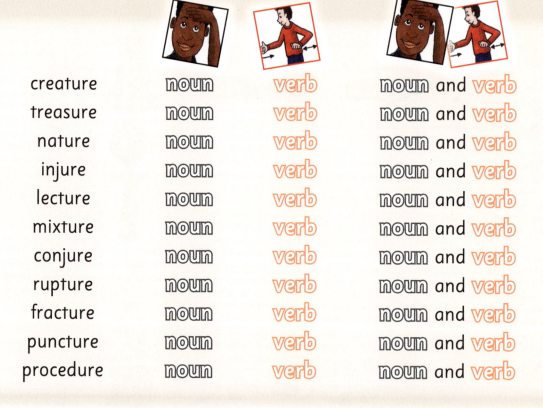

Are these words nouns or verbs or can they be both? Write inside the correct outlined word(s) in black (if it is a noun), red (if it is a verb), or black and red if they can act as both.

creature — noun — verb — noun and verb
treasure — noun — verb — noun and verb
nature — noun — verb — noun and verb
injure — noun — verb — noun and verb
lecture — noun — verb — noun and verb
mixture — noun — verb — noun and verb
conjure — noun — verb — noun and verb
rupture — noun — verb — noun and verb
fracture — noun — verb — noun and verb
puncture — noun — verb — noun and verb
procedure — noun — verb — noun and verb

Parse the sentence and then write it on the wall.

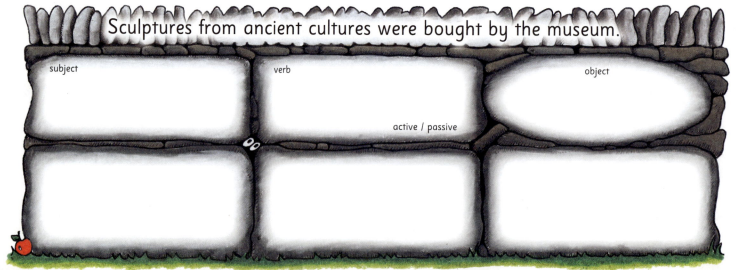

Sculptures from ancient cultures were bought by the museum.

subject | verb | object

active / passive

Positive and Negative Statements

Auxiliary verbs can help to emphasize a positive verb or make it negative. We **stress** the auxiliary for emphasis (You **will** go the party!) and put "**not**" between it and the main verb to make it negative (You will **not** go to the party!). The simple forms of the past and present tenses have no auxiliaries so we use the verb "to do" together with the infinitive form of the main verb instead.

> do/does/did + infinitive = **positive** statement
> do/does/did + **not** + infinitive = **negative** statement

Underline each verb in red and decide whether it is in the past or present tense. Then rewrite each sentence using the correct form of "to do" to a) show emphasis and b) make it negative.

I like bananas.	I do like bananas.	I do not like bananas.
We made pancakes.	We did make pancakes.	We did not make pancakes.
They went home.		
He builds boats.		
You ran away.		
The rain stopped.		
I locked the door.		
You know Sam.		
We met John.		
She plays golf.		
They told you.		
You saw the thief.		

"To do" is often contracted with "not" in everyday speech. Trace over the contractions below and then write them out in full underneath, with no letters missing.

I don't   I don't

I don't	you don't	he doesn't	we don't	they don't

I didn't	you didn't	she didn't	we didn't	they didn't

Dictation: schwa ‹or›

1. _____

2. _____

3. _____

Turn these positive statements into negative statements, using the verb "to do" as an auxiliary, followed by "not" and the infinitive form of the main verb. If the original verb is in the present tense, use "do" or "does," and if it is in the past tense, use "did."

> **do/does/did + not + infinitive = negative statement**

This cheese has an unpleasant odor.
_____

I like this flavor of ice cream.
_____

The ships sailed into the harbor.
_____

They often hear rumors about the old house.
_____

Your neighbor does the gardening every day.
_____

Parse the sentence and then write it on the wall.

The splendid armor was worn by the king in battle.

subject | verb | object

active / passive

Questions and the Verb "To Do"

One way to write a question is to put the auxiliary verb at the beginning of the sentence (**Will** you go to the party?). There are no auxiliaries in the simple past and present tenses so we add "do," "does," or "did" at the beginning instead and put the main verb in its infinitive form.

Rewrite these statements as questions using the verb "to do."

I like bananas more than apples.
Do I like bananas more than apples?

We made pancakes for breakfast.
_____

They went home after the party.
_____

He builds boats for a living.
_____

You ran away from the fierce dog.
_____

The rain stopped during the concert.
_____

Negative questions using "to do" are usually contracted to "don't," "doesn't," and "didn't" in everyday speech. Rewrite these questions, contracting the verb each time.

"Did I not lock the door?" said Dad, anxiously.
"Didn't I lock the door?" said Dad, anxiously.

"Do you not know Sam?" they asked in surprise.
_____

"Did we not meet John two years ago?" I queried.
_____

"Does she not play tennis on Saturdays?" wondered Beth.
_____

"Did they not tell you about their trip?" asked Grandpa.
_____

"Did you not see the thief?" quizzed the police officer.
_____

Dictation: ‹-ity› ‹-ety›

1. _____
   _____
2. _____
   _____
3. _____
   _____

Turn these statements (from page 81) into questions, adding "do," "does," or "did" at the beginning and using the main verb in its infinitive form. If the original verb is in the present tense, use "do" or "does," and if it is in the past tense, use "did."

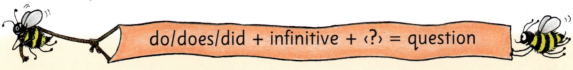

do/does/did + infinitive + ‹?› = question

This cheese has an unpleasant odor.
_____

I like this flavor of ice cream.
_____

The ships sailed into the harbor.
_____

They often hear rumors about the old house.
_____

Your neighbor does the gardening every day.
_____

Parse the sentence and then write it on the wall.

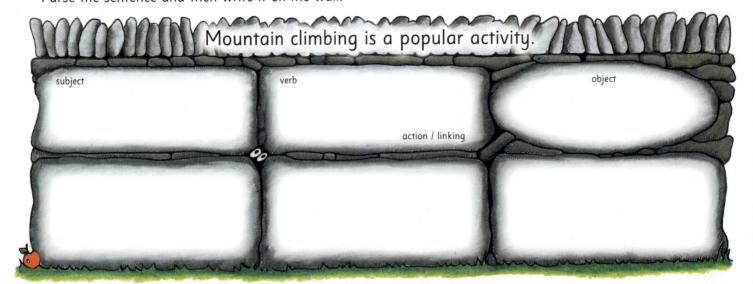

Mountain climbing is a popular activity.

subject | verb | object
action / linking

84

Modal Verbs

Modal verbs are a special kind of auxiliary verb. For example, they can help us express how certain something is, from uncertain (I **might** go to the party) to very certain (I **will** go to the party). Look at each sentence below and decide which definition is correct.

You **could** draw a colorful picture.
- Ⓐ. I suggest that you draw a colorful picture.
- B. I demand that you draw a colorful picture.

She **can** speak three foreign languages.
- A. She wants to speak three foreign languages.
- B. She is able to speak three foreign languages.

He **must** polish his shoes thoroughly.
- A. It is necessary that he polish his shoes thoroughly.
- B. It is optional whether or not he polishes his shoes thoroughly.

If your tongue is numb, you **should** go to the doctor.
- A. If your tongue is numb, I allow you to go to the doctor.
- B. If your tongue is numb, I advise you to go to the doctor.

"We **shall** find the treasure!" cried the buccaneers.
- A. "We are sure to find the treasure!" cried the buccaneers.
- B. "We are likely to find the treasure!" cried the buccaneers.

I said that I **would** make the spaghetti dough today.
- A. I said that I needed to make the spaghetti dough today.
- B. I said that I intended to make the spaghetti dough today.

You **may** leave the table if you finish your fruit juice.
- A. You are allowed to leave the table if you finish your fruit juice.
- B. You are required to leave the table if you finish your fruit juice.

I **will** have another doughnut now.
- A. I am going to have another doughnut now.
- B. I am considering whether or not to have another doughnut now.

They **might** see the rhinos and penguins at the zoo.
- A. It is certain that they will see the rhinos and penguins at the zoo.
- B. It is possible that they will see the rhinos and penguins at the zoo.

‹-ial›

- denial
- trivial
- burial
- jovial
- material
- imperial
- memorial
- territorial
- editorial
- industrial
- secretarial
- ceremonial
- celestial
- sacrificial
- substantial
- marsupial
- prejudicial
- controversial

Work out the answers to the clues and complete the crossword. All of the answers are words in the Spelling List.

1. a statement saying that something is not true
2. used at a formal event which has special traditions
3. large in size or amount
4. relating to the production of things we buy or to things we use, like oil, coal, and steel
5. relating to a religious ceremony where an animal, food, or special item is offered to a god as a gift
6. not important, serious, or valuable
7. the act of putting something in the ground
8. an animal that carries its baby in a pocket of skin
9. relating to the work or skills of an office assistant
10. having a bad effect on something
11. relating to the sky, outer space, or heaven
12. relating to the preparation of a book for printing
13. cheerful and friendly
14. relating to an empire or to the person who rules it
15. something built to remind us of a person or event
16. relating to land owned or controlled by a country
17. cloth used to make things like clothes or curtains

Dictation: ‹-ial›

1. _____

2. _____

3. _____

Which spelling word belongs to the same word family as each of these nouns and verbs?

prejudice	_____	secretary	_____
matter	_____	memory	_____
bury	_____	deny	_____
trivia	_____	edit	_____
sacrifice	_____	empire	_____
ceremony	_____	territory	_____
controversy	_____	substance	_____

Parse the sentence and then write it on the wall.

A memorial service was held for their uncle.

subject — verb — object

active / passive

Adverbs

Modal Adverbs

Like modal verbs, we use adverbs of modality to express how certain we are, ranging from uncertain (**Perhaps** I will go to the party) to very certain (I will **definitely** go to the party).

apparently surely certainly clearly
definitely probably perhaps
obviously maybe possibly absolutely

Modal adverbs can be used with main verbs and modal ones. Identify the modal verbs below and then rewrite the sentences twice, using a different adverb each time. How does the meaning change? Do the adverbs work in some sentences but not in others?

The flavor of the soup could be improved.
___
___

Beth can play the guitar and accordion.
___
___

You must get some medicine for that cough.
___
___

The yacht should be in the harbor.
___
___

The sculpture might be genuine.
___
___

We would visit Thailand in the autumn.
___
___

May I have some new ballet shoes?
___
___

Tom will eat the steak but not the broccoli.
___
___

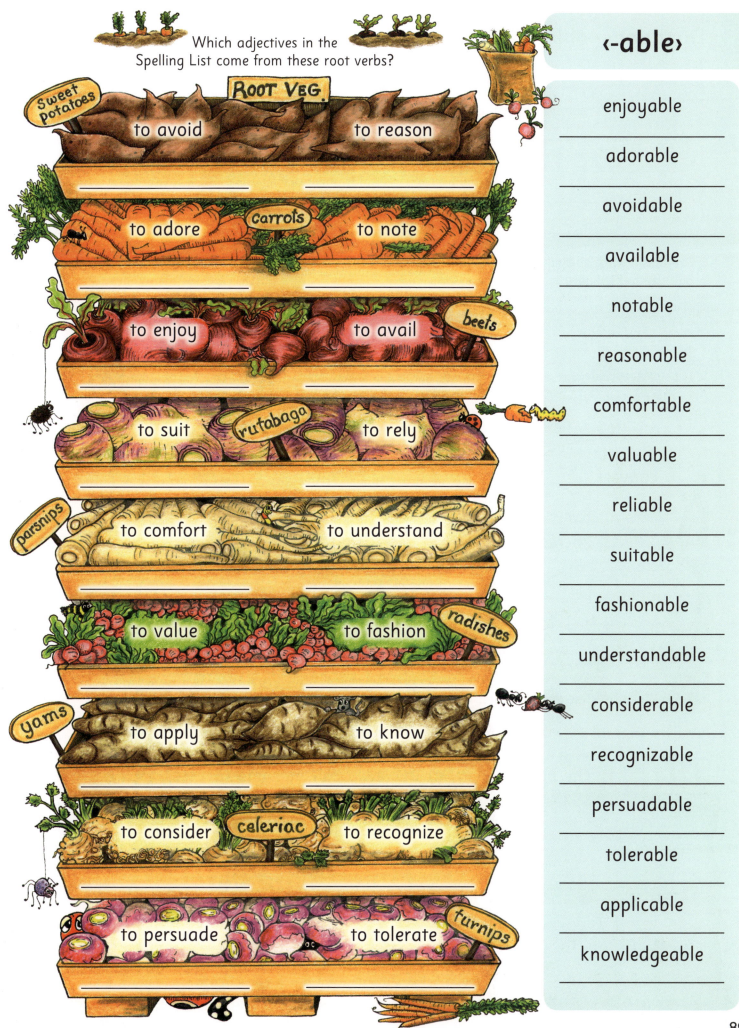

Dictation: ‹-able›

1. _____
2. _____
3. _____

Are these words spelled ‹-able› or ‹-ible›? Add the correct suffix to complete each word, and use a dictionary to check if necessary.

- reli_____
- reason_____
- convert_____
- incred_____
- applic_____
- forc_____
- knowledge_____
- illeg_____
- valu_____
- sens_____
- suit_____
- poss_____

Parse the sentence and then write it on the wall.

The bodybuilder has achieved considerable success.

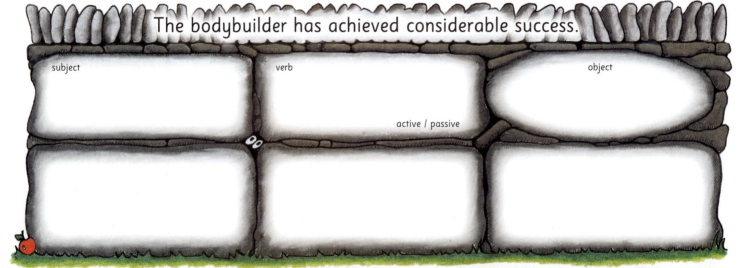

subject | verb | object
active / passive

90

‹que› for /k/

- unique
- antique
- queue
- mosque
- plaque
- conquer
- marquee
- boutique
- physique
- mystique
- opaque
- pique
- grotesque
- picturesque
- masquerade
- statuesque
- technique
- arabesque

 Write a sentence for twelve of the words in the Spelling List.

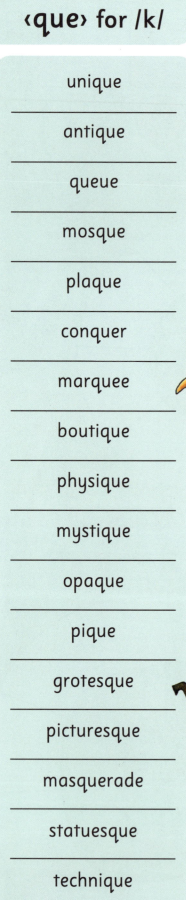

1. ___
2. ___
3. ___
4. ___
5. ___
6. ___
7. ___
8. ___
9. ___
10. ___
11. ___
12. ___

Dictation: ‹que› for /k/

1. _____

2. _____

3. _____

Check what this word means and see how many other words you can make with its letters.

masquerade

Parse the sentence and then write it on the wall.

Many artists have painted this picturesque valley.

subject	verb	object
	active / passive	

Using Paragraphs

Think of something you would like to invent and give it a name. Imagine a) what it could do, b) how you would make it, and c) what the advantages would be. Note down your ideas first on a sheet of paper. Then write about your invention in the boxes below, using some of the linking words and phrases to connect your ideas and help your writing flow from one paragraph to another.

Title:

Introduction

a)

b)

c)

Summary

to begin with	also	alternatively	next	for this reason	to sum up
first of all	similarly	otherwise	then	consequently	finally
at first	in addition	however	later on	accordingly	in short
firstly	as well as	nevertheless	eventually	as a result	after all
secondly	moreover	instead	for example	therefore	on the whole
thirdly	especially	although	in particular	since	in other words
initially	furthermore	even though	meanwhile	so	in conclusion

Find the words from the Spelling List.

```
n b y g o n n o m e n g i n p
i m a b y g i n e f a m m a s
m e d i c i n e x e n u g o n
a h e r o w e x a m i n e n r
g r t u m i g r a i n e n g i
i n e z d e t e r n d o u i n
n e r o i n e v e i h r i u e
e o m a s c u l i n e p n f n
b e i s c i p l n e r t e a g
y x n l i n e b y g o n e m i
g a e x p m i g r a i s h i n
o m d g l c k n t u n d o n e
g e n u i m a o n f e m i e t
v i m a n y o n e q u i n r h
n g o n e s s e m a s c u l i
```

⟨ne⟩ for /n/

one
none
gone
engine
imagine
undone
anyone
famine
heroine
examine
bygone
genuine
medicine
feminine
masculine
discipline
migraine
determined

Which is the correct antonym for each pair of synonyms? Use a thesaurus to help you, if necessary.

1. **false, fake**
    A. undone
    B. determined
    C. genuine

2. **villain, rogue**
    A. famine
    B. heroine
    C. migraine

3. **all, everything**
    A. one
    B. anyone
    C. none

4. **recent, modern**
    A. bygone
    B. feminine
    C. masculine

Dictation: ‹ne› for /n/

1. _____
_____

2. _____
_____

3. _____
_____

Rewrite each imperative twice. First, make it negative by starting with "Do not." Then contract the verb to "don't" and write a sentence with direct speech. Try not to use the verb "to say" each time, but vary it with other verbs, such as "to warn," "to advise," "to instruct," or "to order."

Forget what I told you.
  Do not _____
  "Don't _____

Plant the seeds in large pots.
_____
_____

Come to the house today.
_____
_____

Use the scissors in the drawer.
_____
_____

Take your medicine now.
_____
_____

Parse the sentence and then write it on the wall.

The expert showed us some genuine antiques.

- subject
- verb (action / linking)
- object
- indirect object

Formal and Informal Writing

Write two letters about your invention from page 94. Write a formal letter to a local business who might be interested in making and selling your invention. Then write an informal one, telling a friend all about your plans.

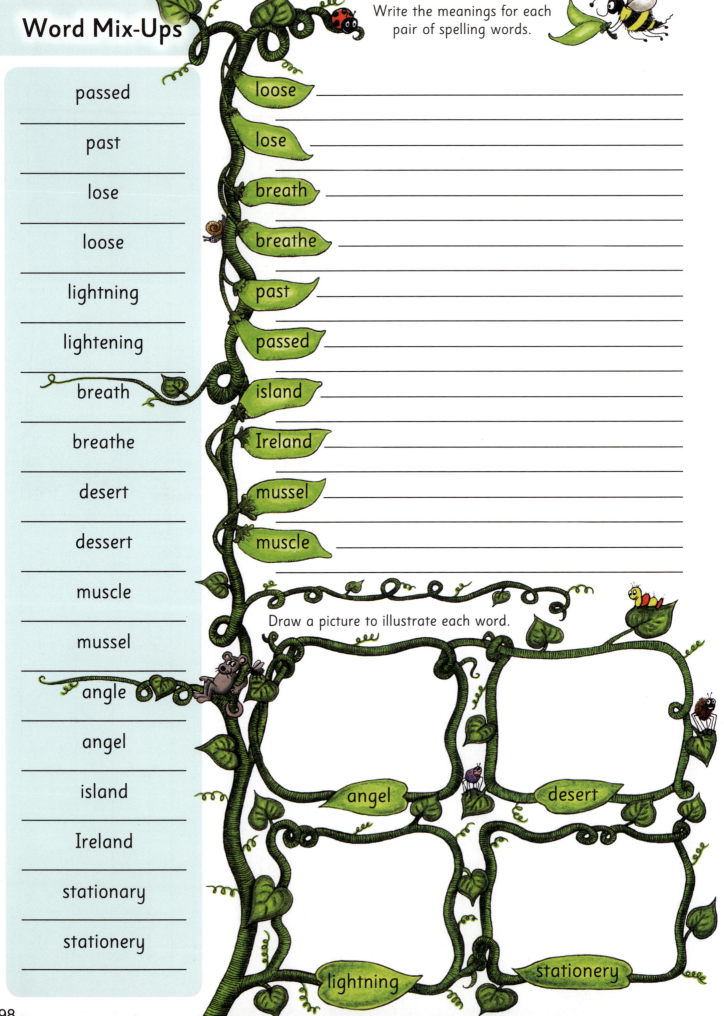

Dictation: word mix-ups

1. _____
_____
2. _____
_____
3. _____
_____

Can you match the formal and informal synonyms below?

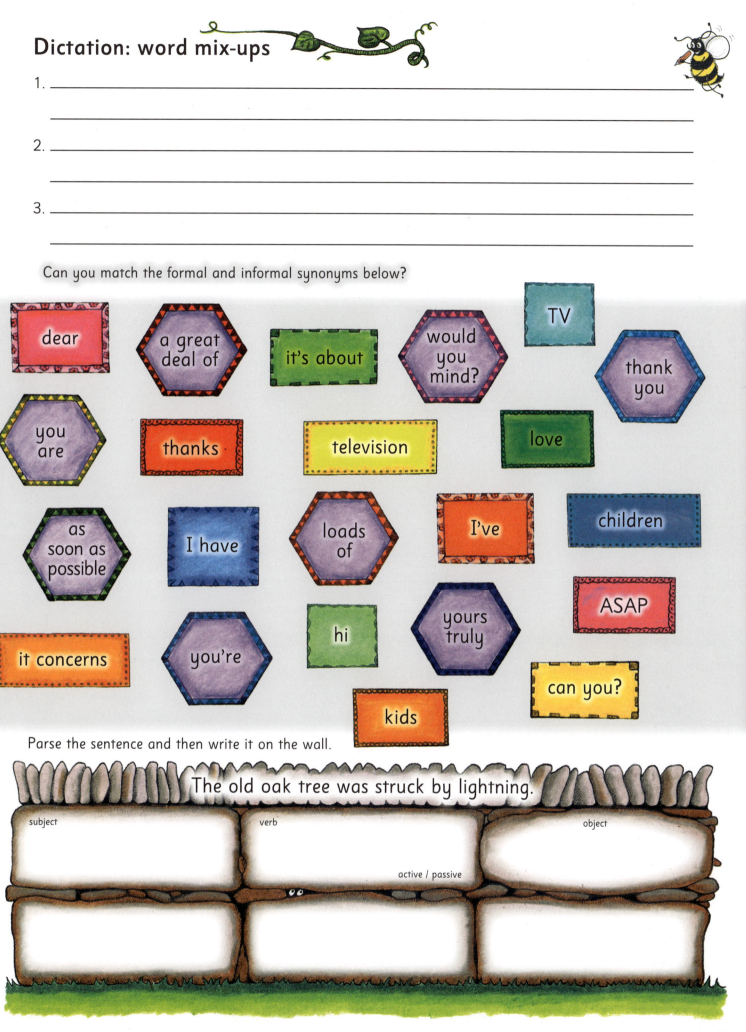

dear	a great deal of	it's about	would you mind?	TV	thank you
you are	thanks	television		love	
as soon as possible	I have	loads of	I've		children
it concerns	you're	hi	yours truly	ASAP	can you?
		kids			

Parse the sentence and then write it on the wall.

The old oak tree was struck by lightning.

subject   verb   object

active / passive

All About Alliteration

She sells seashells on the seashore

ALLITERATION is when we use several words together that begin with the same sound. It gives our writing a certain rhythm, which can be used to create different moods, get the reader's attention, or make something memorable. Alliteration is used to make tongue-twisters and is often found in poetry.

Peter Piper picked a peck of pickled peppers

Write the first letter of your name in the frame and decorate it. Then think of as many words beginning with that letter as you can and write them below. Finally, write a sentence, using as many of the words as possible.

Write an alliterative phrase or sentence using these words.

F — fashionable _____

T — treasure _____

D — doughnut _____

P — penguin _____

G — ghastly _____

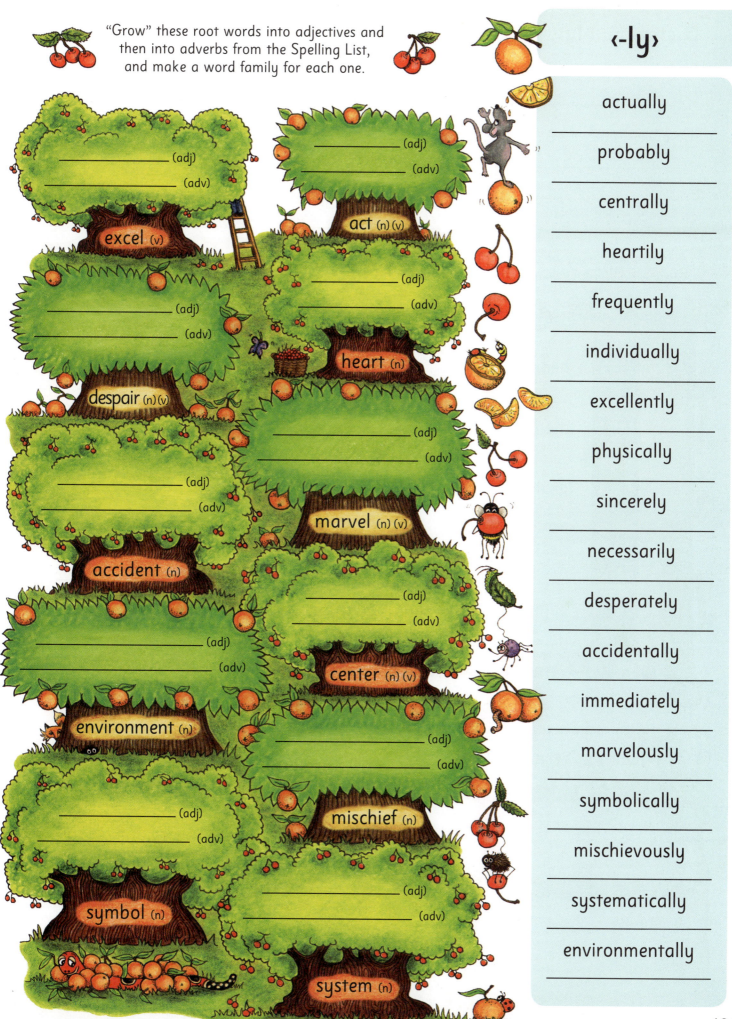

Dictation: ‹-ly›

1. _____

2. _____

3. _____

Alliteration is when we use several words together that begin with the same sound. Write an alliterative sentence for each of these words.

H heartily _____

M medicine _____

G grotesque _____

D dessert _____

C comfortable _____

Parse the sentence and then write it on the wall.

Seth ate his dessert almost immediately.

subject	verb	object
	active / passive	

Dictation: ‹ere› and /oa/

1. _____

2. _____

3. _____

Write the meanings for these commonly confused words. Use a dictionary to check, if needed.

- effect
- affect
- wary
- weary
- accept
- except
- quite
- quiet

Parse the sentence and then write it on the wall.

The soldier had a severely broken toe.

subject | verb | object
active / passive

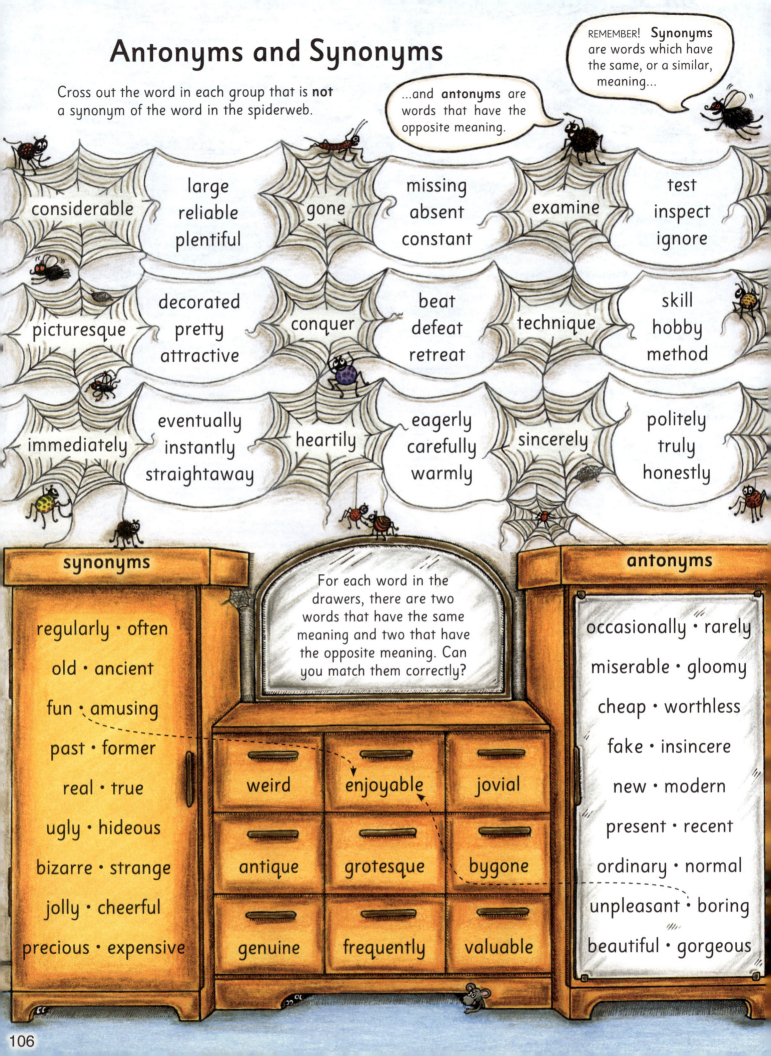

Unscramble the letters to make words from the Spelling List.

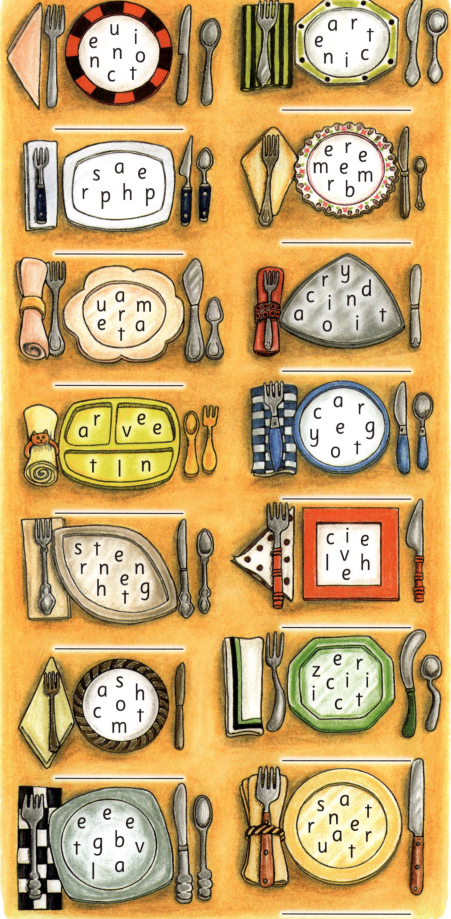
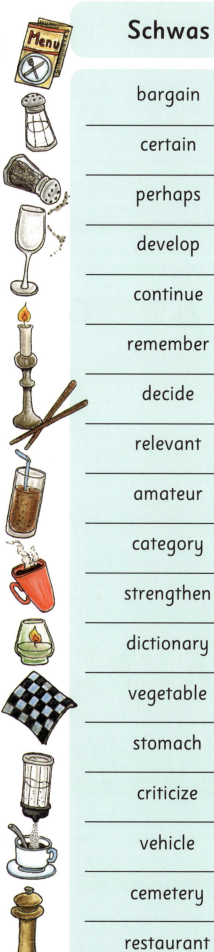

Schwas

bargain

certain

perhaps

develop

continue

remember

decide

relevant

amateur

category

strengthen

dictionary

vegetable

stomach

criticize

vehicle

cemetery

restaurant

Dictation: schwas

1. _____
   _____
2. _____
   _____
3. _____
   _____

Can you think of a fruit or vegetable that starts with each letter of the alphabet? Look in a dictionary or other reference book if you get stuck!

Parse the sentence and then write it on the wall.

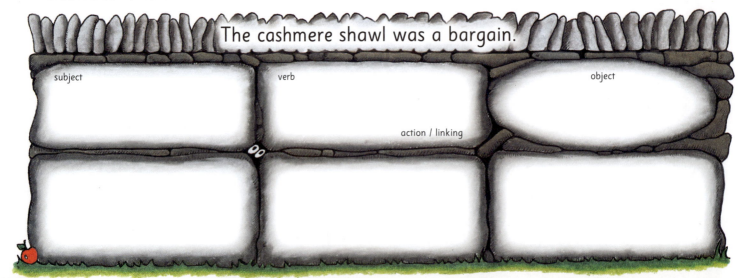

The cashmere shawl was a bargain.

subject | verb | object
action / linking

Trace over the articles, which are listed below. Then think of five words for each part of speech. Remember to write examples of both proper and common nouns.

Articles

a
an
the

Nouns

Pronouns

Adjectives

Verbs

Adverbs

Prepositions

Conjunctions

Now look at the grammar actions below and write a sentence, using a word from each of your lists. Try to choose words that will make sense, although this may not be possible!

GRAMMAR CONSEQUENCES

Spelling Test 1	Spelling Test 2	Spelling Test 3
1.	1.	1.
2.	2.	2.
3.	3.	3.
4.	4.	4.
5.	5.	5.
6.	6.	6.
7.	7.	7.
8.	8.	8.
9.	9.	9.
10.	10.	10.
11.	11.	11.
12.	12.	12.
13.	13.	13.
14.	14.	14.
15.	15.	15.
16.	16.	16.
17.	17.	17.
18.	18.	18.

Spelling Test 4	Spelling Test 5	Spelling Test 6
1.	1.	1.
2.	2.	2.
3.	3.	3.
4.	4.	4.
5.	5.	5.
6.	6.	6.
7.	7.	7.
8.	8.	8.
9.	9.	9.
10.	10.	10.
11.	11.	11.
12.	12.	12.
13.	13.	13.
14.	14.	14.
15.	15.	15.
16.	16.	16.
17.	17.	17.
18.	18.	18.

Spelling Test 7	Spelling Test 8	Spelling Test 9
1.	1.	1.
2.	2.	2.
3.	3.	3.
4.	4.	4.
5.	5.	5.
6.	6.	6.
7.	7.	7.
8.	8.	8.
9.	9.	9.
10.	10.	10.
11.	11.	11.
12.	12.	12.
13.	13.	13.
14.	14.	14.
15.	15.	15.
16.	16.	16.
17.	17.	17.
18.	18.	18.

Spelling Test 10	Spelling Test 11	Spelling Test 12
1.	1.	1.
2.	2.	2.
3.	3.	3.
4.	4.	4.
5.	5.	5.
6.	6.	6.
7.	7.	7.
8.	8.	8.
9.	9.	9.
10.	10.	10.
11.	11.	11.
12.	12.	12.
13.	13.	13.
14.	14.	14.
15.	15.	15.
16.	16.	16.
17.	17.	17.
18.	18.	18.

Spelling Test 13	Spelling Test 14	Spelling Test 15
1.	1.	1.
2.	2.	2.
3.	3.	3.
4.	4.	4.
5.	5.	5.
6.	6.	6.
7.	7.	7.
8.	8.	8.
9.	9.	9.
10.	10.	10.
11.	11.	11.
12.	12.	12.
13.	13.	13.
14.	14.	14.
15.	15.	15.
16.	16.	16.
17.	17.	17.
18.	18.	18.

Spelling Test 16	Spelling Test 17	Spelling Test 18
1.	1.	1.
2.	2.	2.
3.	3.	3.
4.	4.	4.
5.	5.	5.
6.	6.	6.
7.	7.	7.
8.	8.	8.
9.	9.	9.
10.	10.	10.
11.	11.	11.
12.	12.	12.
13.	13.	13.
14.	14.	14.
15.	15.	15.
16.	16.	16.
17.	17.	17.
18.	18.	18.

Spelling Test 19	Spelling Test 20	Spelling Test 21
1.	1.	1.
2.	2.	2.
3.	3.	3.
4.	4.	4.
5.	5.	5.
6.	6.	6.
7.	7.	7.
8.	8.	8.
9.	9.	9.
10.	10.	10.
11.	11.	11.
12.	12.	12.
13.	13.	13.
14.	14.	14.
15.	15.	15.
16.	16.	16.
17.	17.	17.
18.	18.	18.

Spelling Test 22	Spelling Test 23	Spelling Test 24
1.	1.	1.
2.	2.	2.
3.	3.	3.
4.	4.	4.
5.	5.	5.
6.	6.	6.
7.	7.	7.
8.	8.	8.
9.	9.	9.
10.	10.	10.
11.	11.	11.
12.	12.	12.
13.	13.	13.
14.	14.	14.
15.	15.	15.
16.	16.	16.
17.	17.	17.
18.	18.	18.

Spelling Test 25	Spelling Test 26	Spelling Test 27
1.	1.	1.
2.	2.	2.
3.	3.	3.
4.	4.	4.
5.	5.	5.
6.	6.	6.
7.	7.	7.
8.	8.	8.
9.	9.	9.
10.	10.	10.
11.	11.	11.
12.	12.	12.
13.	13.	13.
14.	14.	14.
15.	15.	15.
16.	16.	16.
17.	17.	17.
18.	18.	18.

Spelling Test 28	Spelling Test 29	Spelling Test 30
1.	1.	1.
2.	2.	2.
3.	3.	3.
4.	4.	4.
5.	5.	5.
6.	6.	6.
7.	7.	7.
8.	8.	8.
9.	9.	9.
10.	10.	10.
11.	11.	11.
12.	12.	12.
13.	13.	13.
14.	14.	14.
15.	15.	15.
16.	16.	16.
17.	17.	17.
18.	18.	18.

Spelling Test 31	Spelling Test 32	Spelling Test 33
1.	1.	1.
2.	2.	2.
3.	3.	3.
4.	4.	4.
5.	5.	5.
6.	6.	6.
7.	7.	7.
8.	8.	8.
9.	9.	9.
10.	10.	10.
11.	11.	11.
12.	12.	12.
13.	13.	13.
14.	14.	14.
15.	15.	15.
16.	16.	16.
17.	17.	17.
18.	18.	18.

Spelling Test 34	Spelling Test 35	Spelling Test 36
1.	1.	1.
2.	2.	2.
3.	3.	3.
4.	4.	4.
5.	5.	5.
6.	6.	6.
7.	7.	7.
8.	8.	8.
9.	9.	9.
10.	10.	10.
11.	11.	11.
12.	12.	12.
13.	13.	13.
14.	14.	14.
15.	15.	15.
16.	16.	16.
17.	17.	17.
18.	18.	18.

Formal and Informal Writing

When we speak or write, we think about who we are talking to and what our purpose is, and use words that we think are suitable.

We are usually informal with our family and friends, but use a more formal style when we talk about serious things to important people or to those we do not know.

Look at the more formal words and phrases in the list and match them with the less formal ones in the pyramid.

You could also try making your own large triangle, with new pairs of formal and informal words. Cut it into smaller triangles, mix them up, and then see if you can put it back together again.

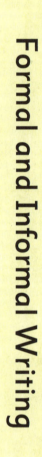

Formal Writing

commence
enquire
assist
discover
you would
I do not
obtain
inform
establish
endeavor
consider
finally
require
demonstrate
apologize
indicate
satisfactory
correspondence

Pyramid (informal words):

letters, show, start, try, find out, ask, point out, get, you'd, think about, need, help, tell, I don't, say sorry, set up, in the end, OK